CW00553406

Modern Turkish Poetry

Modern Turkish Poetry

Edited, translated and introduced by

Feyyaz Kayacan Fergar

with additional translations by

Richard McKane,

Ruth Christie,

Talat S. Halman

and Mevlut Ceylan

The Rockingham Press

1992

Published in 1992
by The Rockingham Press
11 Musley Lane,
Ware, Herts SG12 7EN

Copyright © Feyyaz Fergar 1992
except for poems translated by
© Richard McKane, © Ruth Christie,
© Talat S. Halman and © Mevlut Ceylan

British Library Cataloguing-in-Publication Data

A catalogue record for this book
is available from the British Library

ISBN 1 873468 06 7

Printed in Great Britain
by Bemrose-Shafron (Printers) Ltd., Chester

Printed on Recycled Paper

Acknowledgements

Most of these poems were specially translated over the last three years for this anthology. But some of the translations were published earlier and I would like to express my gratitude to the editors of the following books and magazines for allowing me to reprint them here:

Modern Poetry in Translation, edited by Osman Turkay and Taner Baybars (1971)

Contemporary Turkish Literature, edited by Talat S. Halman in the U.S.A.(1982)

Zenos, editions nos 3 & 4 (1983), edited by Danielle Hope

Core, editions nos 1-4 (1987-1990), edited by Feyyaz Fergar and Mevlut Ceylan

Translation magazine, published by Columbia University, New York (Spring 1989)

"Some Modern Turkish haiku and haikuesque poems" edited by James Kirkup in *Sell,* no 4, published by the University of Kyoto (1987)

"Nazım Hikmet: A Sad State of Freedom", *Greville Press Pamphlets,* edited by Geoffrey Godbert (1990)

Poems of Oktay Rifat, translated by Richard McKane and Ruth Christie, Anvil Press New Poets, edited by Graham Fawcett (1990)

"An Introduction to Modern Turkish Poetry" by Feyyaz Fergar, *Haiku Quarterly* no 4, edited by Kevin Bailey (1991)

CONTENTS

Aşık Veysel *(Ashik Veysel)*
(1893-1975) A contemporary folk poet, born near Sivas in Central Anatolia. He became blind at the age of seven, learned to play the saz (a slim, long-necked lute) and at an early age began to compose poems, which he sang all over Turkey.

Ahmet Hamdi Tanpınar
(1901-62) Author of an excellent history of Turkish Literature in the 19th century. He was also a novelist of considerable talent. But his fame rests on a handful of beautifully written, lapidary poems. Tanpınar wrote like a jeweller, using words with the skill of a diamond cutter. It was not until 1961 that his poems were brought together in a book. Some of his work suggests an affinity with Paul Valéry.

Nazım Hikmet
(1901-63) Born in Salonica, did his primary education at the State Lycée of Galatasaray, founded in the middle of the 19th century where teaching is bilingual in French and Turkish. He attended the Naval School in Istanbul for five years but had to leave because of ill health. He crossed over to Anatolia in order to take part in the War of Independence, Istanbul being under Allied occupation at the time. Stayed in Batum, then went to Moscow to study economics and sociology at the Eastern University

* *In compiling the notes on the poets, I have made extensive use of the biographical data appended by Ataol Behramoğlu to his massive two-volume anthology, "Turkish Poetry of the Last Hundred Years" 1987 (Second Edition 1991). The guide to pronouncing Turkish poets' names is not comprehensive, but indicates where the sound of the consonants is not the same as their English equivalents.*

there. On his return was arrested and sent back to prison at Hopa. Later he worked in Istanbul as a journalist and film-maker; he had his first plays and poems published during this time. He was imprisoned again but set free on the tenth anniversary of the Republic. In 1938 was condemned to a total of 35 years imprisonment by the Tribunals of the War Academy and the Naval Command for incitement to Communism. His sentence was later reduced to 28 years and 4 months. As a result of a campaign at home and demonstrations abroad, he was released under the 1950 amnesty, and spent the rest of his life in exile in Sofia, Warsaw and Moscow, where he died in 1963. His main books of poetry are: "Gioconda and Si-ya-U" 1929, "Why did Benerji Kill Himself?" 1932, "Letters to Taranta Babu" 1935, "The Legend of Sheikh Bedrettin, Judge of Simavna" 1935. In addition to "Letters to his Wife from Prison", he has written a vast series of poems, collected in five volumes under the title, "Human Landscapes from My Country". In "The Legend of Sheikh Bedrettin", Nazım Hikmet wrote a supreme masterpiece which unites with unerring skill the traditions of the Divan (classical) and folk poetry with the achievements of modern verse.

Ercüment Behzat Lav *(Erjüment Behzat Love)*
(1903-84) Born in Istanbul. Went to Berlin to study music and drama. On his return held various jobs as radio announcer, producer at the People's Theatre and lecturer in the Drama Department of the Municipal Conservatoire. He was a leading actor in many early Turkish films. His initial poetry was experimental but in the 1960s he moved closer to Turkish diction. His best poems, with almost Brechtian undertones, are to be found in "Mau Mau", which was contemporary with events in Kenya.

Necip Fazıl *(Nejip Faa-zil)*
(1905-83) His full name was Necip Fazil Kisakürek. Born in Istanbul, he read philosophy at the university there and was given a grant to study in Paris for a year. Afterwards he worked variously as a bank employee, teacher and lecturer. He wrote many plays, one of which ("To Create a Man" 1938) introduced Freudian themes on the Turkish stage. He was a brilliant craftsman and master of syllabist poetry, rising to the height of his genius in books like "Spider Web" (1925), "Pavements" (1928) and "I and Beyond" (1932). He founded the literary magazine, "The Great East" in 1943. But he was gradually engulfed in a didactic mysticism, out of touch with the changing life around him.

Cahit Sıtkı Tarancı *(Jahit Sitki Taranji)*
(1910-56) Born at Diyarbakır in Eastern Turkey. Educated at the French Lycée of St. Joseph in Istanbul and the State Lycée of Galatasaray, he went in 1938 to Paris to continue his studies at the École Libre des Sciences Politiques. By then he was quite a well-known poet. He had a profound influence in bringing new ways of enriching the technique of poetry and was a close friend of the poets who founded the *Garip* (Peculiarist) movement in the late thirties. He had a special affinity with Baudelaire, Verlaine and Jules Supervielle.

Fazıl Hüsnü Dağlarca *(Fazil Hüsnü Dalarja)*
(b. 1914) After Hikmet, the most widely translated Turkish poet of our time. He studied at the Military High School on the Bosphorus and the War Academy and served as an army officer for fifteen years. In 1950 he resigned his commission to devote himself to poetry, and also ran a bookshop and publishing house. He has written more than 70 books, but his fame rests on collections published between 1940 and 1968: "The Child and God" (1940), "The Legend of Çakır" and "The Stone Age" (1945), "Mother Earth" (1950) and "ASU" (1955). In these books man

assumes the stature of myth. In "Haydi" (1968) he produced a cascade of haiku-like quatrains of telling variety. He also wrote politically motivated books like "Hiroshima" (1970).

Orhan Veli

(1914-50) He read philosophy at the University of Istanbul and then worked for the Turkish Post Office and as a literary translator for the Ministry of Education. His main books were "Garip" (meaning "bizarre" or "peculiar") published in 1941 with Oktay Rifat and Melih Cevdet Anday, "Addiction" (1945) and "Like an Epic" (1946). His "Collected Poems" were published in 1982. In the development of Turkish poetry, his achievements should be compared with those of Hikmet. Talking about an erroneous concept of poetry, he said: "we must end the hegemony of 'the line' in poetry. This approach breeds the belief that 'words' are concrete elements of poetry. As a result you have people who look for one hundred kinds of beauty in a poem made up of one hundred words, whereas even a thousand-word poem is written with only one mode of beauty in mind." His direct style was admirably suited to the translation of La Fontaine's Fables, which read as if they were part of the poetic heritage of Turkey.

Oktay Rifat

(1914-88) Born in Trebizond on the Black Sea, son of the poet, Samih Rifat. Completed his studies at the School of Political Sciences in Paris in the late thirties. Switching to Law, he worked for many years as a legal adviser to the Turkish State Railways Administration. Co-author with Orhan Veli and Melih Cevdet Anday of "Garip" (1941), the slim but epoch-making book in the history of modern Turkish poetry. In 1955 he won the Seven Hills Prize for Poetry with his collection, "The Crow and the Fox." After the *tabula rasa* of "Garip", Oktay Rifat is seen here ushering into Turkish a language of lively originality. We observe him using simple, ordinary words of everyday speech as units of an extraordinary syntactic and imaginative world of great depth and brilliance. The result is a magical fable of the human condition. In an interview given soon after the award, Rifat said that "the job of poetry is to find a remedy for social ills." In other words, he held the view that poets were not just spectators but active believers in social responsibility. In a subsequent book, "Freedom has Hands" (1966), he brings his lyrical powers and the strength of his social awareness into play in order to underline his concern for the human and political questions that always dominate the conscience of man. In his later work, Oktay Rifat wrote masterfully short poems, giving us an insight into his world of love, life, freedom and hope. These cameo-like poems encapsulate vast vistas of feeling and thought. He was also the author of many novels and successfully staged plays.

Melih Cevdet Anday *(Melih Jevdet Anday)*
(b. 1915) Educated in Turkey, went to Brussels for two years to study sociology but was forced to return home on the outbreak of the Second World War. He lectured on drama and diction in the Conservatoire of Istanbul. His weekly articles in the national daily *Cumhuriyet* were eagerly received and won him a large following. Co-founder with Orhan Veli and Oktay Rifat of the Garip school of poetry, he also wrote some successful plays. His books of poetry include "The Tree that Lost its Mind" (1946), "The Telegraph Office" (1952) and "Side by Side" (1956) which caused him to be prosecuted under Article 142 of the Turkish Penal Code. With later books like "Odysseus Bound" (1963), "On the Nomad Sea" (1970) and "The Legend of Gilgamesh" (1981) he came into his own as a "thinker-poet", but some of these poems are top-heavy with symbolism and allegory.

Müştak Erenüs *(Müshtak E-renoos)*
(b. 1915) Studied law at the University of Istanbul and is a practising lawyer. His cameo-like poems reveal a biting sense of humour with a lyrical twist.

İlhan Berk
(b. 1916) Like Özdemir Ince, he is a graduate of the French Department of the Atatürk Education Institute. Worked in the Press Bureau of the Bank of Agriculture until his retirement. Has published more than 20 volumes of poetry and translated, among others, Rimbaud and Lorca. İlhan Berk has always been in the forefront of the innovative movements and has been awarded most of Turkey's literary prizes. He has developed a pure, sunny, flowing style with deft touches of colour. Some of his short poems read like burrowing feelers into nature. One can detect the influence of Walt Whitman and St. John Perse in his large-scale poetry.

Behçet Necatigil *(Behchet Nejatigil)*
(1916-79) Born in Istanbul, he studied and taught Turkish literature. He published skilful translations of Wolfgang Borchert and Knut Hamsun and left a vast body of poetry. In books like "The Covered Bazaar" (1945), "Houses" (1953), "Threadbare Earth" (1956), "A Bunch of Poems" (1965), "To Walk Alone and with Oneself" (1968), "Zebra" (1973) and his posthumously published poems, Necatigil like Orhan Veli dwells on the little, timorous man facing the daily jabbing blows of fate. His poems with their broken, hesitant lines sound like glass shattering in the mind. He brings to life the little man's obsessions with a life in which he has only his resignation to fall back on. But there is, nevertheless, something inspiring in these short poems, something reminiscent of a Kafkaesque Merlin in search of an articulate alchemy. The prestigious Necatigil Prize for Poetry was instituted by his family in 1980 after the poet's death.

Cahit Külebi *(Jahit Külebi)*
(b. 1917) Graduate of the Faculty of Turkish Language and Literature of the Teachers' College for Higher Education. Served for a number of years as Cultural Attaché at various Turkish embassies abroad. His most famous collection of poems is "Atatürk in the War of Independence" (1952). Another collection, "Green is the Grass" in 1955 won him the

Poetry Prize of the Turkish Language Academy. His poems, some bitter, some bright, seem to have been distilled from the best of Turkish folksongs.

Salah Birsel
(b. 1919) Graduate of the University of Istanbul's Faculty of Philosophy. He has held various jobs: chief librarian, head of the Ankara University Press, editor-in-chief of the monthly review of literature of the Turkish Language Academy. He is now a freelance writer in Istanbul. The roots of his poetry lie in the rich and pithy traditions of Turkish satire and folk humour. He is also a brilliant essayist and chronicler.

Feyyaz Kayacan *(Fey-yaaz Kayajaan)*
(b. 1919) The nom-de-plume of the editor of this anthology, Feyyaz Fergar. Born in Istanbul, educated at the Jesuit-run Lycée of St Joseph, he went to study politics and economics in Paris (1938-39) and Durham University (1940-44). He joined the BBC External Services in 1946, retiring in 1979 as Head of the Turkish Section. His book, "Shelter", gathered together stories based on his experiences of the London Blitz, and in 1963 won the short story prize of the Turkish Language Academy. Reviewing it, Professor Talat Halman wrote: "Reading Kayacan is a hypnotic experience: very few Turkish writers nowadays can boast of a style as lilting and incantatory as Kayacan's". This poetic book of prose has been credited with inspiring a new movement in language and style among the young poets of the fifties and sixties. In his two collections of poems - "A Spoon to Feed my Hunger" (1976) and "My Spider is Different" (1982) - Kayacan developed a compact style of looking at things.

Sabahattin Kudret Aksal

(b. 1920) Studied philosophy at the University of Istanbul and worked as a teacher and manager in municipal theatres. His collected poems won the prestigious Seven Hills Prize in 1980. He is a successful short story writer and playwright, and his play "Mr. Nihil" was successfully performed in Istanbul in 1991. He has also translated Paul Éluard into Turkish. Though his early work tended to be repetitious, he arrived in time at an elliptical, impressionistic way of seeing and saying things. His poems may be defined as deep-running watercolour paintings - some of them sound like pure Zen.

Necati Cumalı *(Nejati Joomaali)*

(b. 1921) Graduate of the Faculty of Law of Ankara University, he was for many years a barrister but gave up his practice to devote himself to literature. He has written many short stories, novels and plays, many of these successfully staged in translation in a variety of languages. He may be said to be a confessional poet in so far as his personal life is sometimes reflected in his work, but he more often deals with social problems. In "The Light Beautiful" (1951) he looks at ordinary people, life in remote provinces and the shady corners of a town, in other words the sorrows of life. The dominant note here is a kind of sad, bleeding lyricism. But Cumalı can also produce lilting poems full of the joys and hopes of living, and here he deals with nature and memories of the past and childhood. In his later work, "A Horseman in the Steppe" (1981), intellect takes over from the effusions of the heart and he uses themes like nature, history, time to reach a widening perception of reality.

Özdemir Asaf

(1923-81) Studied Law and Economics at Istanbul University and worked for various insurance companies before starting a publishing house. In books like "The World Caught My Eye", "The Sides of the Circle", "How are You?", "You, You, You" and "Don't Eat the Flowers", he gives us mostly short poems which read like a "string of brilliant colourful proverbs or apophthegms". He displays in them his gift for impish wisdom and uses the same gift for a confrontation with what is dark, ugly and devious in the world.

Arif Damar

(b. 1925) Went to school in Istanbul. For a long time, he ran a bookshop. His collection of poems, "Cloud of Istanbul", was awarded the Seven Hills Prize for Poetry in 1958. In 1988 he published his ninth book entitled "We were Poor and We Fell in Love with the World" and in 1990 almost his entire output was collected in two large volumes. A socialist poet of the forties, Damar for a while fell under the influence of the Second Renewal Movement but in his latest poems, which have appeared in magazines, we see him moving closer to a spare, bright and lyrical style.

Attila İlhan

(b. 1925) Studied Law in Istanbul and lived in Paris for six years. A leading figure in contemporary Turkish literature, he has written outstanding works of fiction, essays, travel books and film scenarios. He is the winner of many awards. In his poetry, İlhan shows himself a master of many techniques, at home in the spirit of both the folk and divan (classical) poetry. His six years in France enhanced the scope of his poetic skills. His discovery of Nazım Hikmet whilst still a student at the lycée led to many confrontations with the police. İlhan's poetry is full of brilliant, romantic imagery, rich in verbal innovations. But his romanticism never loses sight of the social ills and problems that weigh on the mind and life of man. His main books are: "Boulevard in the Fog" (1954), "Fugitive from the Rain" (1955) and "Diary of a Man under Arrest", which in 1973 won the Poetry Prize of the Turkish Language Academy.

Ahmet Arif

(1926-91) Born in Diyarbakır in Eastern Turkey. In 1950 he was accused of actions detrimental to the peace of the land and arrested under article 141 of the Turkish Penal Code. In 1952 he was re-arrested and served a two-year prison sentence. On his release, he settled in Ankara where he worked as a journalist. His poems were published throughout the forties and fifties but then suffered neglect. On their re-issue in book form in 1968, he achieved a resounding success. The book, "I Wore off Chains and Shackles for the Love of You", has so far sold more than 30,000 copies - an event of the same magnitude as the tumultuous reception given to the re-publication of Nazım Hikmet's poetry.

Can Yücel *(Jaan Yüjel)*

(b. 1926) Born in Istanbul, the son of Turkey's greatest Minister of Education, Hasan Ali Yücel. Read classics at the University of Ankara and then Cambridge. He was for almost five years a programme assistant in the Turkish Section of the BBC External Services. He is a man of vast knowledge and culture, as well as keen political and social awareness. He is a superb translator of Shakespeare, Emily Dickinson, Auden, Eliot, Dylan Thomas and the Greek epigrammatic poets. His poetry thrives on a strong combination of lyricism, warm irony and sarcasm. This quality is especially evident in his "Poems of a Political Prisoner" (1974). His other collections are "Wall of Love" (1973), "Death and My Son" (1976), "The Music of Colours" (1982), "The Steep Heaven" (1984), "Life Offering" (1986) and "The Child Colours the Man" (1988). Can Yücel has earned himself a leading place in today's Turkish poetry as a man who upholds what is bright and what gives hope and courage to life. He says jovially, in his big-chested baritone voice: "I've never been awarded a prize, only a prison sentence."

Hasan Hüseyin

(1927-84) Studied Turkish literature in Ankara and then worked as a petition-writer for the illiterate, and as a sign-painter and proof-reader. In many of his poems, he raises his voice in defence of ordinary working people, particularly in his collections "Kavel" (1964), "A White Dove on my Black Handcuffs" (1974) and "The Seeds are Buried in Salt" (1988). These works contain some of his strongest poems. Hasan Hüseyin wrote in an epic, sweeping style which showed the influence of Nazım Hikmet and Attila İlhan. His lyrical temperament worked hand in hand with an acerbic sense of humour, which increased the "hitting power" of his poetry.

Turgut Uyar

(1927-85) Born in Ankara, like F.H. Dağlarca, he came to poetry via the Army. Resigning his commission in 1958, he worked in the Ankara offices of the Cellulose and Paper Consortium. His first books show the influence of Cahit Sıtkı Tarancı, Orhan Veli and Attila İlhan, but in 1959 with "The Loveliest Arabia in the World" he found his own powerful, rich and individual voice. In 1963 he won the major Seven Hills Prize for Poetry with "The Tobaccos are Wet". Although we can detect in these works the presence of Dağlarca, Uyar writes with a rarely matched sureness of touch and vision, using daring and felicitous image and word combinations.

Metin Eloğlu *(Metin Elolu)*

(1927-85) Born in Istanbul, he studied painting at the Academy of Fine Arts. He has published many books of poetry. In the first of these he tends to favour the language of the man in the street and the argot of those on the shadowy fringes of town. We then follow him switching to a sharp-edged delivery, akin to the voice of Nazım Hikmet. In his more successful poems, we can also find traces of the influence of Orhan Veli, where he savours the beauty and liveliness of everyday Turkish - "the slang of the heart". He is at his best when he gets close to Can Yücel and Cemal Süreya in poems that are full of irony but readily responsive to the human condition.

Edip Cansever *(Edip Jaansevair)*
(1928-85) Studied at the High Institute of Commercial Studies, then opened and ran an antiques shop in Istanbul's Covered Bazaar. He was one of the leading members of the young generation of poets who in the fifties created a new poetic diction and a new world of imagery. He was awarded three of Turkey's most important poetry prizes. His important collections include "Gravitational Carnation", "The Park of Lost Hopes", and "Where is Antigone?" Ataol Behramoglu, the poet and anthologist, says of him: "In *Where is Antigone?* we come across obvious signs of Eliot's influence". Cansever's work was many-sided and he came under many influences, which enriched his development towards a very personal and mature style.

Cemal Süreya *(Jemaal Süreya)*
(1931-90) Born in Erzincan of Kurdish parents and studied at the School of Political Sciences in Ankara. Was for a number of years an Inspector of the Inland Revenue and also served as Director of the Mint. His first book, "Uverjinka" (1959, which won the Seven Hills award) caused quite a stir. Here was a new voice, complex and complicated but simple and flowing at the same time. In his next two books - "Nomad" (1966, Poetry Prize of the Turkish Language Academy) and "Kiss Me and Bring Me into the World" (1973) - he achieved a greater depth of love and understanding, of tenderness and warm irony. What is best in his work was collected in "Worlds of Love" (1984) and this will endure. Cemal Süreya was also a critic and essayist of great acumen and subtlety. His book of criticism, "A Hatful of Flowers", is a pleasure to read. He also edited - on and off from 1961 until 1970 - an influential literary magazine called "Papirus",

which featured contributions from the leading poets and writers of the country. He died in Istanbul in a diabetic coma.

Talat Sait Halman

(b. 1931) Born in Istanbul and a graduate of the American Robert College on the Bosphorus. An indefatigable and brilliant champion of Turkish poetry in the United States, where he has taught Turkish language and literature at the universities of Columbia in New York and Princeton, he published a massive anthology "Contemporary Turkish Literature" in 1982. Talat Halman served as Turkey's first Minister of Culture in 1971. He is also a poet in his own right who in the last few years has written poems of deep and subtle significance.

Ece Ayhan *(Éjé Ayhan)*

(b. 1931) Like Cemal Süreya, was a graduate of the School of Political Sciences in Ankara; he later worked as an officer in the provincial administration. A daring innovator, he uses language not as a rational word-carrier - but as an instrument to unveil new insights into the world of visions. He says: "Poetry is one of the exits of imagination." In this respect, it is interesting that his essays, collected in a book in 1987, bear the title "Armless Calligrapher". Ayhan's other books are "The Seas of Mrs. Kinar" (1959), "The Black Cat with Unseeing Eyes" (1965), "Orthodoxies" (1968) and "State and Nature" (1973). When he avoids the pitfalls of excessive linguistic fantasies, Ayhan reaches the stature of a poet who puts us in touch with the searching anxieties and sorrows of man. This happens convincingly in his book, "State of Nature", his masterpiece.

Sezai Karakoç *(Sezai Karakoch)*
(b. 1933) Born in Ergani in Eastern Turkey and, after university, worked as a Treasury Controller, an Inspector in the Inland Revenue, a columnist and publisher. His first poems were published in conservative magazines and he edited a review called "Rebirth", indicating his closeness to Islamic mysticism. Karakoç, like Cahit Zarifoğlu and İsmet Özel, aims at bridging traditional Islamic beliefs and modern poetic techniques.

Gülten Akın
(b. 1933) Turkey's outstanding woman poet. She studied law at the University of Ankara and then worked as a barrister in several parts of Anatolia where her husband held administrative jobs. She won the Poetry Prize of the Turkish Language Academy in 1961 and again in 1971. She has a calm, strong voice, deeply embedded in the sinewy language of ordinary people, in the sad and joyful songs that form the treasury of Turkey's folk culture. In some of her poems, we observe her moving close to Nazim Hikmet. Gülten Akın has taken her place in the forefront of poets for whom poetry is synonymous with social responsibility.

Cevat Çapan *(Jévat Chapaan)*
(b. 1933) Studied English Literature at Cambridge and, returning to Turkey, was appointed in 1974 Professor of English Literature at Istanbul University. He also taught Drama at the State Academy of Fine Arts. He is known for his deft translations from English, American and Greek poets. His own poems have been collected in two volumes. The first, "Return of the Dove", won the renowned Necatigil Prize, and was followed by a second, "Natural History."

Hilmi Yavuz *(Hilmi Yavooz)*
(b. 1936) Born in Istanbul, studied law for a while. In the late fifties, was a founder member of "A", an influential poetry broadsheet publishing the works of the emerging young poets of the movement known as the Second Renewal. In the middle sixties, he worked as a programme assistant in the Turkish Section of the BBC and holds an honours degree in philosophy from London University. He is Cultural Adviser to the Mayor of Istanbul and in 1991 organised a Poetry Symposium, the first international poetry festival ever to be held in Turkey. He has also published a book of translations from Neruda. The poetry of Hilmi Yavuz has many dimensions, many polarities. The hallmarks of his art are a committed concern for the ideals of justice and freedom, and probings into the deeper levels of poetic consciousness. He has won many literary prizes.

Kemal Özer
(b. 1936) Studied Turkish literature at Istanbul University and worked for many years as a proof-reader. He published a magazine called "The Art of Poetry" and was also in charge of the old-established literary magazine, "Varlık". In 1976, he was awarded the Poetry Prize of the Turkish Language Academy. He was among the poets who developed a socially-loaded poetic voice in the immediate wake of the Second Renewal movement. With his book, "The Poetry of the Days We Live In" (1974), he moved on to join hands with the leftist poets. But his poetry is free of the jargon of raucous slogans and dedicated to the humanity of liberty.

Özdemir İnce *(Özdemeer Injé)*
(b. 1936) Graduate of the French Language department of the Atatürk Education Institute, he studied for a year in Paris and worked also as a teacher and translator. He translated into Turkish the poems of Yannis Ritsos, the Greek communist poet, and for this was awarded the Turkish Language Academy's Translation Prize in 1979. He wrote a book on

"Poetry and Realism" and between 1986-87, in collaboration with Ataol Behramoglu, produced a four volume "Anthology of World Poetry". His familiarity with the French surrealists has enabled him to achieve greater freedom of expression - under the control of a sharp mind. The influence of Nazim Hikmet is evident in his work.

Ülkü Tamer
(b. 1937) Educated at the American Robert College in Istanbul, he went on to study at the Institute of Journalism. For a while he worked as an actor, and then became editor-in-chief of the literary monthly, "Arts on the Move" published by the newspaper *Milliyet.* He has written seven books of poetry and was awarded the prestigious Seven Hills prize with his book, "What I Inhale is Not Air but the Sky" (1966). Tamer is a skilful translator of poetry and prose, mostly American. At his best, he has given memorable examples of both the purely lyrical and socially committed poetry.

Ergin Günçe *(Ergin Gunché)*
(1938-83) Born in Giresun on the Black Sea coast, he studied at the School of Economics and Political Sciences in Ankara and then went to Paris to prepare his Ph. D. He then joined the teaching staff of the Middle Eastern Technical University in Ankara. He died in an air crash. The title of his first book, "To Die Young" (1966) seems clairvoyant in retrospect. His collected poems were published soon after his death. Günçe's poetry is reminiscent of Lorca's flowing and ardent lyricism, coloured by a deep concern for social problems.

Cahit Zarifoğlu *(Jahit Zarifoloo)*
(1940-87) Studied German Literature at the University of Istanbul and then worked for TRT (Turkish Radio and Television) as a broadcaster and translator. Zarifoğlu's poetry oscillates between the diaphanous and the

hermetic. He edited a magazine called "Mavera", which aimed to establish a link between Islamic tradition and a modern, progressive style in poetry.

Egemen Berköz

(b. 1941) Has a degree in Italian Language and Literature and works as a copy-writer in an advertising agency. With his broken lines, his staccato diction, combined with impressionistic undertones, he stands close to the low-keyed poetry of Behçet Necatigil. Berköz represents the ordinary, sensitive man, trying to exorcise the anxieties of everyday life.

Melisa Gürpınar

(b. 1941) Poet, short story writer and drama critic. In the sixties she came to England as an au-pair to learn English and during her stay broadcast for the BBC Turkish Service many lively reviews of the London theatre. Back in Turkey she has been actively involved in promoting the arts and has recently been appointed Secretary-General of the Turkish Writers' Union.

Ataol Behramoğlu

(b. 1942) Studied Russian at Ankara University, and then spent four years of further study in England, France and the Soviet Union. As a result of the trials associated with the Peace Movement in 1982, he spent ten months in a detention camp. In 1984, he went to Paris where he attended seminars at the Centre for the Study of Comparative Poetry and contributed translations of Turkish poetry to a magazine called "Phoenix". Later in the eighties, he produced a two-volume anthology entitled "Turkish Poetry of the Last Hundred Years". His articles on the principles of art and literature were published in 1991 under the title "Mechanical Tears". The main books of his own poetry are "An Armenian General" (1965), "One Day Without Doubt" (1970), "Poems of Love, Courage and Struggle" (1974), "Quatrains" (1980) and "Letters to My Daughter" (1991). He has also produced translations of Russian poetry and fiction.

İsmet Özel

(b. 1944) Attended the School of Political Sciences in Ankara, then switched to the study of French and now teaches French at the State Conservatoire in Istanbul. Together with Ataol Behramoğlu founded and edited the magazine, "Friends of the People". His best known collections are "Rebellion, Yes" (1969), "Book of Murders" (1975) and "When I was Smiling at My Executioner" (1984). With his aggressive lyricism, he spearheaded a new awareness of social responsibilities. But in the seventies, he moved away from his previous stand towards a mystical view of life, without losing the strength of expression and inventiveness which he had evolved during his socialist period.

Güven Turan

(b. 1944) Studied English Literature at Ankara University and later attended seminars in Creative Writing at the University of Iowa. He has developed a style which avoids the meandering longeurs of poetry. He writes short, flicking, almost jabbing poems which are all the more sharp-edged for their conciseness. They read like a shorthand rendition of deep-seated feelings and fugitive states of anxiety. Turan is a prize-winning novelist, an essayist and a university lecturer on language communication.

Özkan Mert *(Özkaan Mért)*

(b. 1944) Born in Erzurum in Eastern Turkey. After High School, he studied Turkish literature for a while at Ankara University. He now lives in Stockholm, where he works for the Turkish Service of Swedish Radio. His collected poems appeared in 1988. Mert's poetry is socialist to the core without the excesses of total obedience. His poems rise to the skies like sturdy kites.

Refik Durbaş *(Refik Durbash)*
(b. 1944) One of the finest of the young socialist poets who came to prominence in the seventies, moving away from the excesses of the Second Renewal movement towards poetry committed to social responsibility. His outstanding books are "Moonlight in My Cell" (1974), "Where Does the Sky Fly to?" (1983) and "Abyss is his Address" (1987). Durbas's language is warm, direct and sustained by the strength of objectiveness. He has enriched the poetry of his generation with the depth and beauty of his own imagery and diction. He has won two of the most coveted poetry prizes in Turkey - the Seven Hills Prize (1979) and the Necatigil Award (1983).

Sennur Sezer
(b. 1944) Had to abandon her High School education to work as a bookkeeper, and was for a while an editorial assistant on the staff of *Varlık*, Turkey's oldest literary magazine. She has also worked for the newspapers *Cumhuriyet* and *Hürriyet*. Sennur Sezer has published seven books of poetry, the last two being "Cards of Identity" and "Who are the People in this Picture". She is a woman with a strong social conscience, expressing itself in sensitive, sometimes bitter tones.

Nihat Behram
(b. 1946) Born in Kars in Eastern Turkey, he studied at the Institute for Advanced Journalism. Accused of actions judged detrimental to national stability, he was arrested in 1972 and imprisoned. He founded with his elder brother (Ataol Behramoğlu) the magazine "Militant". He has lived abroad since 1980 and published two books in West Germany, where he received a grant from a fund set up by the family of Heinrich Böll and the

Ministry of Culture. In 1987 a selection of his poems were published in Turkey under the title "Smiling All The Same".

Ismail Uyaroğlu
(b. 1948) Graduate of the Institute of Education in Istanbul, he taught in various schools and was for a while a journalist. He then joined the Writers' Cooperative "Yazko". His poems were collected in 1985 in a book entitled "From Inside the Fire". In his later work, he evolved a conciseness of expression which lent his voice greater penetration. Uyaroglu's children's books have been well received and his play, "The Carrion", won first prize at the Antalya International Festival of the Arts in 1977.

Bariş Pirhasan *(Barish Peerhasaan)*
(b. 1951) Born in Istanbul and studied English at the University of the Bosphorus. He belongs to Turkey's second generation of post-1960 socialist poets and his sharp-edged imagination stems from an extensive study of poetry. He has published two books of poems, "History is Evil" (1981) and "Anonymous Manuscripts" (1985).

Turan Koç *(Turaan Koch)*
(b. 1952) Lives in Kayseri where he teaches philosophy in the Faculty of Theology. One of the "Muslim Poets" who derive their images from the Islamic values which dominate their approach to the world. He has published two books of poems. Koç is a romantic poet - a haunting sadness sometimes steals into his work - and yet he also possesses a realistic imagination and contrives to create a unitary vision of the world in his poems.

Arif Ay *(Aa-rif Eye)*
(b. 1953) Studied Turkish literature and Islamic theology at Ankara University and currently works as an adviser for the Department of Family Planning. He has published six books of poems and for ten years has edited a magazine called *Edebiyat* ("Literature"). One of the group known as the "Muslim poets", revolutionary themes lie at the heart of his inspiration and sharp images increase the impact of his poems.

Tuğrul Tanyol *(Too-rool Taan-yol)*
(b. 1953) Born in Istanbul, and educated at the Catholic Lycée of St Joseph and the University of the Bosphorus. He is now a lecturer in the Social Sciences Department of the University of Marmara, also in Istanbul. He has three books of poems to his credit, one of which won the Necatigil Prize in 1985. Tanyol has found the way of synchronising strength of thought with sensitive observation. Though his imagery tends at times to be almost surrealistic, it is tightly controlled by a taste for classical conciseness. He has come to be looked upon as a spokesman for his generation and the promise in his early work is borne out by his latest collection, "Chamber Music", published in January 1992.

Yaşar Miraç *(Yaa-shar Miraach)*
(b. 1953) Born in Trebizond on the Black Sea, after High School he went to Germany and then returned to study Turkish Literature at Ankara University. He founded a publishing house called "The New Song" and his first book of poems, "The Young Man of Trebizond" won the Poetry Prize of the Turkish Language Academy in 1980. In the same year he produced "The Rose and the Bread", in which his theme was the problematic lives of peasants and workers, to which he brought a new breath of colour. Another book, "The Silver Sea of the Roses of Peace" in 1986 won the Abdi İpekchi Peace and Friendship Prize, named after the well-known assassinated newspaper editor.

Hüseyin Avni Dede

(b. 1954) Born in Istanbul where he attended High School. He is the epitome of Bohemianism, with his long beard and torrential hair, and he tries to make a living by selling his books on street stalls. These books, with titles like "The Dead Play the Violin" and "Pain is Bullet-Proof", reveal him to be a likeable, straight-forward and out-spoken romantic. A selection of his poems has been translated by Richard McKane and published under the title of "Byzantine Coffin Nails".

Mevlut Ceylan *(Mev-lut Jai-laan)*

(b. 1958) Another of the group identified as "Muslim poets", he has published six collections. Also translated into Turkish works by contemporary Urdu and Bengali poets as well as James Joyce and Mahmoud Darwish. He now lives in London where, in collaboration with Feyyaz Fergar, he founded the international poetry magazine, "Core", with special emphasis on Turkish poets.

Nevzat Çelik *(Nev-zaat Che-lik)*

(b. 1961) He was a first year Graphic Arts student in Istanbul when he was arrested in 1980 for alleged involvement in the activities of the extreme leftist organisation, Dev-Sol. Consequently, he spent many years in prison and faced a possible death sentence. He was not set free until 1987 after his first books of poems, "The Song of Dawn", won the Poetry Prize of the Turkish Language Academy in 1984 and an enthusiastic reception had been given to his second book, "The Song of the Lifer". Çelik's obvious sources of inspiration are Nazım Hikmet and Ahmet Arif. What makes his work so interesting is the artless sincerity with which he brings the elements of his daily life into his poetry. Excerpts of his work were translated into English by Richard McKane and published in the journal, "Index on Censorship". Some of Çelik's poems have now been set to music and recorded by Ahmet Kaya, the popular Turkish folk singer.

Necati Polat *(Nejati Polaat)*
(b. 1962) Another member of the group of poets with socio-mystical inclinations. In some of his poems he uses a facetious, light tone to veil the anger and anxiety which flow beneath the surface of his work. Although undoubtedly inspired by Islam, Polat is far from being a proselytiser. He is a lecturer in philosophy.

Kemal Kalé
(1960-90) Born in Istanbul, with a progressively crippling muscular disease which condemned him to a wheelchair from the age of 11. He could not even finish primary school and his education was completed at home. But his love of poetry manifested itself in his childhood years and his poems were soon published in some of the country's leading magazines. Kemal Kalé countered his bitter physical handicap with a deep fealty to life and the uplifting climate of poetry.

Editor's note:

With the exception of two longer poems by Nazım Hikmet and Ismet Özel, I have opted for shorter poems in this anthology. For the longer poems of Oktay Rifat, Melih Cevdet Anday, Attila İlhan, Necati Cumalı, İlhan Berk, Ataol Behramoğlu and Turgut Uyar, readers are referred to "The Penguin Book of Turkish Verse", edited by Nermin Menemencioğlu in collaboration with Fahir İz (London 1978).

INTRODUCTION
by Feyyaz Kayacan Fergar

"We have the Magna Carta but no cuisine," said an English friend of mine some years ago. He came back from a visit to Turkey smacking his lips in memory of all the succulent dishes with which he had 'enlightened' his palate. He added: "I met an extraordinary man in Istanbul. He wore glasses, false teeth and a toupet. But there was nothing false about his dazzling mastery of the art of Turkish cooking. He said he could cook for me lunch and dinner for three months without repeating himself once." I believed him implicitly. Items like "nightingale's nest", "beloved's lip" and "woman's thigh" have an exciting poetic aura and their recipes should be re-written by a modern John Donne or Andrew Marvell. When I told him that Turkey had its own Donnes and Marvells and a rich poetic tradition kept alive today by the works of outstanding poets, he gave me such a voluminous look of utter disbelief that I decided not to pursue the matter any further. I had a different man, a different person in front of me.

History conditions memory and manipulates feelings. For a saddeningly large number of people the word *Turk* triggers off a set of echolalic images, such as the sword-brandishing janissary invader, the grave-worthy body of the sick man of Europe or the pot-bellied, lethargic hubble-bubble smoker. It is sometimes difficult to reject the idea that all history does is to teach prejudice, hatred and malice; that is to say the clichés that sustain and propel dark, traditionally blinkered emotions. It can be argued that history books bulge with concentration camps wherein to herd supposedly non-grata nations. In such cases it becomes necessary to form escape committees to relieve "the dark in the midst of blazing noon" and shed light on the past of peoples whose undeniable achievements have been obscured or belittled by a persistent lack of understanding.

The virtues of Ottoman administration were conveniently swept aside, although not by all. There were some exceptions, mostly diplomats of distinction, who were impressed by what they saw and expressed their admiration in no uncertain terms. Amongst these we must mention Ogier Ghiselin de Busbecq, who was Imperial Ambassador at Constantinople between 1554 -1562. De Busbecq, dwelling on the system of meritocracy prevalent in the Ottoman Empire had this to say: "Those who receive the highest office from the Sultan are for the most part the sons of shepherds and herdsmen and, far from being ashamed of their parentage, they actually glory in it and consider it a matter for boasting that they owe nothing to the accident of birth ... With us there is no opening left for merit. Birth is the standard for everything, the prestige of birth is the sole key to advancement in public service." *(Translated by Paul Coles)* *

Paolo Giovio in his work, *Turcicarum Rerum Commentarius*, written in 1539, voices the opinion that in severity and justice the military discipline of the Ottomans surpassed that of the ancient Greeks and Romans. The Turks might have been an awesome foe in the field of battle, but toleration was the hallmark of their attitude towards religion. Nobody tried to emulate the night of St. Bartholomew; God was not made an instrument of bloody purposes. It must have been the religious carnage in France which prompted Jean Bodin, the author of the *Six Books of the Republic* (1576) to write: "The King of the Turks, who rules over the great part of Europe, safeguarded the rites of religion as well as any prince in this world. Yet he constrains no one, but, on the contrary, permits everyone to live according as his own conscience dictates. What is more, even in his seraglio he permits the practice of four diverse religions: that of the Jews, the Christian according to the Roman rite and according to the Greek rite, and that of Islam." By the time Jean Bodin was writing, the Ottoman Empire controlled Greece and the Balkans and had expanded westwards through Serbia and Hungary, while Süleyman the Magnificent had added to his long list of titles that of Caliph - successor to the Prophet Muhammet.

There were no pass laws in the Ottoman Empire. There was no Inquisition, no pogroms either. It was the Turks who eventually opened their doors to the Jews, the wandering race, expelled by the Iberian powers and their inhuman, implacable Church. Some of these Jews who found a haven in Salonica and Constantinople were destined to rise to eminence in Ottoman affairs, notably Joseph Nasi who for services rendered in diplomacy and commerce was declared Duke of Naxos by Sultan Selim II.

Of all the arts that contributed to the growth of Turkish culture, poetry is the most important and enjoys a long and sustained tradition. The roots of Turkish poetry stretch back to shamanistic times: the earliest Turkish poems were epics singing the heroic deeds of nomadic tribes from the steppes of Asia and constitute the original treasury of oral literature. Migrating westward in the ninth century into the Caucasus and Anatolia, the Turks came under the spell of a superior civilisation, that of Islam. The impact of

* *Unless otherwise indicated, the translations of all the quotations in this Introduction are by the editor.*

Islamic culture resulted in a new form of poetic practice known as Divan Poetry. This is a highly sophisticated, stylised, over-ornate genre written by a few for a few. It is the poetry of the élite and written in Ottoman Turkish, that is mostly in Arabic and Persian with a few Turkish words thrown in to play a supportive part. Turkish was really treated as a second-class citizen. The Divan Poetry is the poetry of the Empire, voicing the high, relaxed aspirations of the conservative establishment. It was imposed from above. It was the court poetry. Many of the Sultans themselves were accomplished poets. Süleyman the Magnificent, under the pen-name of Muhibbî, wrote some beautiful verse with the genuine lyricism of a love inspired by his non-Moslem wife Roxelane, known in history as Hürrem Sultan. Two of the greatest Ottoman poets, Fuzûlî and Bâkî, lived in the reign of Süleyman who was a truly magnificent patron of the arts.

The mystic folk poetry tradition which, parallel to the Divan prosody, represents the other, equally rich facet of Turkish poetry, cultivated and developed the indigenous themes that underlined the genius of Turkish culture since before the advent of Islam. It had a freedom, a liveliness of its own and did not suffer from the strait-jacket of the poetic discipline which was to spell the ruin of the classical Arab-Persian style. But Islamic mysticism was still an intrinsic part of Turkish folk poetry. Yunus Emre was probably its greatest representative. He was a worthy contemporary of Mevlana Jelaleddin Rumi, the great master of sufi thinking and poetry, and also of Dante Alighieri. Both Dante and Y. Emre died in 1321. But Yunus Emre had something that we do not find in the stern aloofness of Dante's *Divine Comedy*. That is the wonderful sense of humour that colours the pragmatic mysticism he displays in his dealing with his own god. Yunus Emre is not a supine worshipper. He can take Allah to task to plead the cause of man. Listen to him apostrophising his Maker:

> You set a scale to weigh deeds, for your aim
> is to hurl me into Hell's crackling flame.
>
> A scale is suitable for a grocer,
> for a small merchant or a jeweller.
>
> Sin, though, is the vilest, filthiest vice,
> the profit of those unworthy of Grace.
> You see everything, you know me fine,
> then why must you weigh all these deeds of mine?

God Almighty, why all this talk, why must
we prattle about a handful of dust?
Translated by Talat S. Halman

Yunus Emre, in another poem - as if to say "what would you have done had you been in my boots?" - reproaches God in these daring but endearing terms:

Oh Lord, you created a bridge, hair-thin
and you said "whoever can cross this bridge
shall achieve the perfection of heaven on earth".

Dear God, millions of us have fallen off it
in the attempt. I am now going to sit back
and ask you to cross the bridge of your own making.

The miraculous thing is that Yunus Emre's Turkish is so modern and has the dynamism and pithiness of a language that registers with contemporary immediacy and impact. Whereas we find it hard to understand some of the poems written by Yahya Kemal Beyatlı (1884-1958) in the spirit of the neo-classical school.

Now to go back to the Divan Poetry. In the early decades of the 18th century, Nedim, the elegant genius of the Tulip Era, tried to inject real life and spirit into the body of classical prosody by resorting more often to the use of the Turkish language, themes and imagery. The only poet who could have brought to fruition what Nedim had started was Sheikh Galip. But he was unable to revitalise Ottoman poetry and instead retreated into a kind of verse redolent of borrowed mystical philosophy. With his death in 1799, decadence was set in motion. Excessive mimicry, continuous dependence on Arabic and Persian predecessors led Turkish poets into a morass of dead-ends. The depth and gracefulness of stylisation which had flourished in the hands of great poets gave way to a state of stagnation and desiccation in the works of versifiers. The monotony of imagery had a strangling effect on poetic vision. Writing had become a game of transfers. Poets had muzzled themselves with irremediably static themes - all that could be done was to churn out variations on themes defunct. The alembic of inspiration had nothing to distil. The rose which was always mobilised to address the beloved, to describe her lips, her cheeks, was now the tombstone of love. One is reminded here of William Blake's sick rose. But this particular rose was beyond any doctoring - it was not even good for jam-making. The classical genre of poetry went hobbling on into the 19th century which saw the emergence of a hybrid oriental-occidental view. The dominant culture was French culture. "Paris had replaced Shiraz," wrote E.J.W. Gibb, the historian of Ottoman literature.

What brought about the need for re-orientation was the vicious circle Divan Poetry had been engulfed in. One cannot progress in a vacuum, one cannot force a nation to speak with a voice not its own. The élite that produced this particular culture having become stultified, Divan poetry lost all relevance, whereas the tradition of folk poetry is still alive today. We can hear its echoes reverberating through the works of modern Turkish poets. When after the collapse of the Empire the need to assert a cultural identity made itself felt again, the poet-sociologist Ziya Gökalp formulated the way to literary recovery. Gökalp was never to achieve greatness as a poet but he knew that the poetic north was to be found in folk poetry. These are his memorable words: "We belong to the Turkish Nation, the Islamic community and Western civilisation. Our literature must go to the people and at the same time towards the West."

Amongst the poets of the 20th century who upheld and enriched the voice of Turkish poetry, Nazım Hikmet holds a place of seminal importance. There were elements who did not agree with *his way* of going to the people, but the irrefutable fact is that he infused the language with a new breath stressing the simplicity and powerful directness of the Turkish language. With him also, free verse came into its own in a vigorous fashion. In this respect we can detect the influence of Tevfik Fikret, a late 19th century Turkish poet who mobilised the resources of free verse in his fiery political and social diatribes. Some of Hikmet's early poems are marred by a rather vociferous and raw imitation of Mayakovsky. He had come into contact with the latter's work when he was studying in the early twenties at the University of the East in Moscow. But he was to free himself gradually and achieved an intensity of diction rarely matched in this century. He became the poet of vast human compassions. I think it is right to say that in terms of outlook and inner make-up he stands closer to Neruda than Mayakovsky. For him life is always the business at hand. This is how he puts it in his poem "About Living":

> Yes, you'll take life so seriously
> that even at seventy you'll plant olive trees.
> *Translated by Richard McKane*

He has this to say on the same theme:

I mean however and wherever we are, let's be there ...
This earth ... like an empty walnut will roll
in the pitch black of infinity ...
To feel the pain right now,
to feel the depression here and now.
Translated by Richard McKane

Hikmet must also have been acquainted with the work of the great French surrealist lyricist Paul Éluard. I may be wrong but some of the poems he wrote in prison for his wife Pirayé read like pure Éluard, the Éluard of "Poésie et Vérité". That feeling is especially reinforced when we read Hikmet's poem dated 24th September 1945:

The best sea: has yet to be crossed
the best child: has yet to be born
the best days: have yet to be lived ...
Translated by Richard McKane.

The second linguistic shake-up occurred during the late thirties, a period of feverish cultural ferment in Turkey. All the major works of world literature - ancient, classical and modern - were being translated and published with sustained regularity. The magazine "Translation", published by the Ministry of Education, provided work for many young writers including Orhan Veli and Melih Cevdet Anday and opened many, many new doors for its avid readers.

This was the period which saw the birth of the movement known as *Garip* (later to be called the First New, though I would opt for "New Beginning"). *Garip* in Turkish stands for many things. It can mean strange, alienated, lonely or even peculiar. Let us pick up this last attribute and say that the trio of young poets - Orhan Veli, Oktay Rifat and Melih Cevdet - who had unfurled the banner of this new rebellion really wanted to appear peculiar. Theirs was the poetry of peculiarism. There was no mistaking their intentions. They were not going to toe any established lines. They had stripped language down to its barest essentials. In the late thirties they had initiated a minimalist poetry whose counterpart in Europe would take years to mature. The poetry of understatement which came on the literary scene in England with the New Lines anthology looks elephantine compared with the short, darting poems of the *Garip* period. Here for instance is one, outstanding in the accuracy of its aim. It was written by Melih Cevdet Anday and it is entitled: "The Map of Heaven":

Listen to me, my immortal soul,
when I die remember not to go
winging your way up to heaven.
The Big Bear is there, and the Little Bear,
the Scorpion, the Snake, the Centipede,
the Ox and the Bull:
they're all up there
Stay put my soul,
heaven is no place for you.

Now we can see the uninterrupted line of tradition stretching from the Yunus Emre of the 1320s all the way to the middle of the twentieth century. The Map of Heaven is, in many ways, the replica of the hair-thin bridge. Melih Cevdet Anday must also have written this poem under the aegis of Yunus Emre's telling line:

Too many words are fit for the beast of burden
Translated by Talat S. Halman

What the poets of *Garip* did was to bring poetry down to earth by taking out of it what was shoddily poetic, by removing the viscosity of sticky, sugary words and images which caused poems to get stuck on their outward journey. In this context, I would like to quote a line from an early poem by Oktay Rifat entitled "The Raven". The poem is directionless, but the line itself is a solid body blow against sentimentality:

I would like to smell an unusual flower but
I am afraid it might be a rose.

I am surprised it has not been singled out before.

La Fontaine, a great fabulist but hardly a great poet, knew the necessity of keeping things tidy. He called it "écheniller le jardin des Muses". It is a very apt image. One ought to grow flowers in one's garden, not quicksands. The *Garip* poets had early in their writing career come under the influence of the French surrealists. But what appealed to them was not the verbal outrages of André Breton's automatic writing but the lyrical tenderness and depth of Éluard's scintillating imagery expressed through an almost lapidary simplicity. Oktay and I were students in Paris just before the last war. I remember him quoting to me quite often a very short poem by Philippe Soupault (another surrealist poet, whose claim to fame rests also on his translation of Joyce's Ulysses into French).

Monsieur Miroir marchand d'habits
est mort hier soir à Paris.
Il fait nuit
il fait noir
il fait nuit-noire à Paris.

It is not the surrealist nature of the poem that Oktay was interested in but its very down-to-earth, almost pedestrian simplicity and the warmth of its sadness. Talking about death and things to wear, Oktay Rifat was a good-looking man, always well-dressed, always clean. His constant prayer was: "Dear God, let there be no holes in my socks if I die unprepared". But he was not afraid of death. When they asked Hemingway what is death, the reply was "just another whore". Oktay's approach was different. For him death was "a twin brother and a universal spoil-sport, all rolled into one".

Here by Orhan Veli, the moving spirit of Garip, is a poem that sounds like a tongue-in-cheek epitaph for half of mankind:

For the Fatherland

Oh all the things we have done for our fatherland!
Some of us died
some of us delivered speeches.

This poem is a clear-cut example of Orhan Veli's naked, almost wordless approach to poetry. He went even further than Zbigniew Herbert to achieve a strict economy of lyricism. Both Oktay Rifat and M.C. Anday were in a way using Veli's language. It was therefore natural for them to "build" their own individual voices. Oktay Rifat developed a rich and deeply-fluent style, reminiscent of Matisse's drawings and paintings, whilst Anday went to tackle subjects of an intellectual and philosophical nature in his long and successful epic poems like "Odysseus Bound."

Most modern Turkish poets have in one way or another been influenced by European literature, especially the French poets of the nineteenth century like Baudelaire, Verlaine, Rimbaud and Mallarmé. Ahmet Haşim was to introduce his own version of French symbolism early in this century. Yahya Kemal Beyatlı, who brilliantly upheld in the broad daylight of the twentieth century the traditions of the classical divan poetry with his prestigiously colourful and panoramic poems, had in his youth felt a kinship with the work of the equally colourful Hispano-French Parnassian poet, José Maria de Heredia. He too painted in his poems vibrant historical frescoes, the most famous of them following the exploits of the Conquistadors.

But Fazıl Hüsnü Dağlarca's development followed a totally different path. He never came within the orbit of any of these poets. He knew no foreign languages. His poetry therefore bears no trace of borrowing of any kind. His voice was Turkish-bound. His poetic sensibilities and vision were shaped by the geography and sound of the Turkish tongue. This was to be a threshold from which Dağlarca, the monoglot poet, would advance towards the depths of a diction which are uniquely his own. He was the architect of the third linguistic revolution. He created a new, surging dialect out of the very veins and ores embedded in the voice of his country. Dağlarca's poetry reminds one at times of rock-formations, of sculptured insights into wind, light and water. He has the power of vision encompassing the great and the minute alike. In one of his poems called "Audience" echoing the grandeur of the Ottoman past, he confronts us with an imaginary ruler who proclaims:

> ... Here in my white hands
> the dawn of my people begins.
> Noble, strong, handsome and absolute
> as far as the mind can conjecture
> I am Halim the Third.
> Mountains everywhere who are you?

Yet the arrogant beauty of this accent can give way to a deep feeling of loving understanding. Here is a short poem, translated by Talat Halman:

> the widow's cat
> is warmer
> than the bride's cat.

The poetry of Dağlarca has a quality which, for want of a better definition might be called "dark singing simplicity". This in the sense that Lorca used the adjective "dark" - his *duende*. Sometimes he comes up with questions which leave us with alternating feelings of plenitude and anxiety:

> Stop now. All the mothers have given birth.
> Who then is pregnant?

Dağlarca's poems are full of mysterious tropisms, stirrings. You feel them germinating, intent upon outcome and arrival, seeking sun-carrying words or breathing through stone and leaf. He has also written some of the most beautiful poems on childhood. He brings to life the world of the child with all its luminosity, its magic, its joys and hurts. Love must act quickly, therefore he says:

go child, go and pray
before your hands get dirty.

Of his committed poetry, *Mother Earth* is among the best. In it he rejoins the shining tradition of the old folk poets and raises his virile voice to express his fellow-feelings for the peasants. It could be said that he was thinking of them when he wrote, in another book, these four short lines:

As loaves
diminish
our hands
grow. *(Translated by Talat S. Halman)*

He becomes earth and seed, plough and plant. In his hands the most ordinary utensils and tools acquire grail-like qualities. His is the voice of man's pride and dignity. In his *Agony of the West,* he dismisses religious discrimination and addresses Jesus:

Like a hunted animal
your body lies stretched on the cross.
But your time, in all directions,
dwells in us.
Your palms enduring in this world
declare that we are friends.

In a sequence of poems entitled *Hiroshima,* Dağlarca takes his stand in no uncertain manner against American war policy and speaks through the voice of the pilot who unleashed history's first atom bomb:

I pulled the lever and Hiroshima the flower
petalled off into extinction. How can that be?
Where did I gather these multiples of death?
My mind becomes a fire-bird and erupts
into dark, dark flights.

Dağlarca later went on to write a book which he called *Our Vietnam War.* He was a regular officer in the Turkish Army but resigned his commission to devote his life entirely to poetry. He knew what the business of war was all about. He knows that - I'm quoting again from his *Hiroshima* sequence

Living is as sacred as the sky is blue
Living cannot be committed to earth.

He has the generosity of heart of a man who believes that man was meant to achieve and to live by the holy ordinance of peace and love. He feels moved to ask that humanity be granted

> not the day of judgment
> but the day of understanding.

This reflects a sense of mission that most writers and poets in Turkey share - just like the Russian authors of the 19th century. When I was at school in the Lycée St. Joseph in Istanbul, I remember our teacher of Turkish literature, Tevfik Hodja, saying to us: "Children, the highest court of justice in Turkey is poetry."

Few are the younger modern Turkish poets who were not indebted to Dağlarca. One of these is Behçet Necatigil. But the influence here is linguistic and stylistic. Necatigil's world is different. He burrows like a mole in the dark minutiae of life. His poems are like miniature domes under which reverberate inscrutable intimations of mortality. In *Lines of Death,* he tells us:

> Love calls with many voices, cajoling and coy,
> each a multiple of her mask ...
> Then the curtain goes up once more:
> will this river flow for me again?
> Something is wrong, something is missing
> to be alive is still the thing.

There is a Kafkaesque presence in these furtive lines. Necatigil seems to say to us: let us be grateful for the minutest of mercies - being in a dead-end is better than being dead.

In contrast, the poetry of Turgut Uyar, Edip Cansever, Cemal Süreya, İlhan Berk, Ülkü Tamer, Ece Ayhan and Hilmi Yavuz is full of colour, movement, spaciousness and innovative spirit. These voices, together with lesser ones were grouped under the name of *Ikinci Yeni* - The Second New. I would like to translate this as the Second Renewal, because it sounds less literal and closer to English.

No Ordinary Table, one of the most memorable poems produced by this school, was written by Edip Cansever. Its meaning is more slippery than a bevy of eels. We have a man who uses a table seemingly as a receptacle or repository for his earthly possessions - but it also contains his dreams, his hopes, his likes and dislikes, his sleeping and his awakening. He is a kind of conveyor-belt piling on the table the modalities of his existence. He is doing all this "in the midst of the joy of living". We are not really sure whether the table represents the counter of a pawn shop, the preface to a momentous testament or just a dustbin. But as the title suggests, this was no ordinary table:

> It was not put out by such a load.
> It swayed once or twice then steadied itself.
> The man went on adding.

Can Yücel does not fit into any movement or school. But his caustic wit is always alert, always on the prowl. He is a worthy modern counterpart of Nef'î, the great master satirist of the seventeenth century. His *Lament for a Geranium* is a dark Lorcaesque parody-cum-allegory in which the colour of a geranium arouses the escalating suspicions of the prison authorities and the flower is arrested "at five o'clock in the afternoon". This poem has earned itself an altogether different niche in contemporary Turkish poetry. Attila İlhan, the author of a successful trilogy of novels, also proved himself to be a brilliant lyrical-realist poet, who can incorporate slang and folksy proverbs into the texture of his poems where he makes skilful use of both old and modern forms of poetic metres and techniques. His work has been extensively anthologised.

Attention must be drawn to poets who came to achieve prominence in the wake of the movement of Second Renewal. They are Ataol Behramoğlu, Hasan Hüseyin, İsmet Özel, Özdemir İnce, Arif Damar, Refik Durbaş, Özkan Mert and Kemal Özer. They are all lyrical poets with unswerving dedication to the spirit of love, justice, freedom and humanity. Of these, Ataol Behramoğlu, İsmet Özel and Hasan Hüseyin can be said to have inherited Nazim Hikmet's burning epic diction in their longer poems.

Tugrul Tanyol and Güven Turan are two poets who maintain a spirit of inquisitive alertness, alive to the pitfalls of blind ideological allegiances. Güven Turan has chiselled himself a clipped, tense approach which owes a lot to his ability to use words with creative restraint. Tugrul Tanyol, a younger contemporary of Turan - and an academic by profession, teaching sociology - seems to combine a deep sense of lyrical serenity with the promptings of a clear, probing mind. He looks set for greater things and his latest book, *Chamber Music*, published in January 1992 shows that he is on the move.

I have enriched this anthology with a special section devoted to the works of a new "breed" of authors who call themselves "Moslem poets" to underline that faith is the mainspring of their inspiration. The poets in question are Sezai Karakoç, Cahit Zarifoğlu, Arif Ay, Turhan Koç, Necati Polat, Mevlut Ceylan and İsmet Özel the greatest of them all. Reading them, one develops the conviction that they echo the genuine strength and humanity of living faith. I myself cannot imagine them giving way to the dark excesses of fundamentalism. Their beliefs are deeply traditional but their technique and imagery is avant-garde, almost experimental.

This anthology closes with three diminutive poems from the work of Kemal Kalé, a gifted young poet whose brief life was spent in the grip of an unforgiving, painful disease of bone and muscle. I met him at the Hatay, a famous Istanbul taverna close to the Marmara Sea, where poets and writers sign their books, where painters exhibit their latest pictures, and knowledgeable customers fraternise with friendly and spirited bottles of raki. Kemal had been chair-bound since the age of nine and he was wheeled in by his lovely and devoted sister. He signed for me a copy of his second collection entitled *Ageless Climates* and the date was 25th June 1989. Browsing through the pages I came across the lines:

> The day I die wear a green dress,
> forget my face, forget my hands,
> go and walk in singing fields
> and hang my name
> on the branch of a great old tree ....

He must have seen me reading. "I, too, like that poem," he said. He added later: "Will you please let me know what you think of my poems. Tell me what is good in them, tell me also what they lack. Because one tends to grow fond of one's shortcomings and look upon them as achievements." Kemal Kalé could have led the life - mental and physical - of a cripple. The discovery of poetry in his early teens restored to him a different kind of freedom of movement, a different sense of mobility. The above quotation shows that few poets have applauded life and love with such gusto, courage and fortitude. After my return to London, I corresponded with him for a while. When I went back to Turkey in the summer of the following year, he rang me at the house of some friends where I normally stay - but I was out. The message was late in reaching me. Three days later - it was June 1990 - he died. Why did he ring me? Did he have something to ask or something urgent to say? I'll always wonder. Literature is the domain of passing fads and fancies. I don't know whether Kemal Kalé will achieve the reputation I feel he deserves, but at least I want him to make his presence felt in this book.

London, 1992

Aşık Veysel
(1893-1973)

LET FRIENDS REMEMBER ME

I go and my name stays.
Let friends remember me.
A wedding, a holiday,
let friends remember me.

The soul does not stay in a cage, it flies away.
The world is a caravanserai where one settles then moves off,
the moon goes round, years pass,
let friends remember me.

The soul will depart from the body,
the chimney does not smoke and the fire does not burn.
Let there be armfuls of selams,
let friends remember me.

I would neither have come nor gone,
day by day my troubles mount up.
My place and my village stay desolate,
let friends remember me.

All sorts of flowers blossom and die.
Who has laughed and who will laugh?
Happiness is a lie and death a truth,
let friends remember me.

It's afternoon then the evening comes.
See what happens to one.
Veysel goes, his name stays,
let friends remember me.

Translated by Richard McKane

Ahmed Hamdi Tanpınar
(1901-62)

BEYOND TIME

I am
not within time,
nor entirely beyond;
but in the flux
of an all-embracing, complete, indivisible moment.

All forms in a trance
of strange dream-tones,
even a windblown feather
is not as light as I.

My head a vast mill,
grinding out silence;
my heart a dervish
naked of cloak or goatskin,
who has reached his desire.

I perceive
the world become
a creeping ivy, rooted in me;
I swim at the centre
of a deep blue light.

Translated by Ruth Christie

ONE DAY IN ICADIYE

One day
in Sultantepe or Icadiye
a melody takes wing,
and suddenly where you are
a universe opens,
enchanted, endless, free.
Washed in the wind of today
the rose of the past
one by one scatters its leaves
in the well of your dreams.
Now you'll look with a different eye
on the sleep you call 'life'.

Perhaps the strangest legends you have heard,
the dawn-kingdom in the branchy woods,
old stoic pines alone on every skyline,
evenings that leak away like secrets from your life,
yearly advent of hawthorn and chestnut,
and in their crumbling graves the dreaming dead -
- all will be born again
to the love you thought dead;
and you'll know the only death
is the passing of time.

LAST OF THE LOOT

Everyone helps themselves to a share of the loot,
the wind steals our voice,
the sun our shadow....
and our thoughts stay behind,
caught in the net of the stars.

Translated by Ruth Christie

THE BLACK HORSES

One day
the cold wind of night in your hair
you'll close down these horizons
silent and weary you'll wait in your corner
for the black horses of your final journey.

And softly you'll say to yourself,
'I'm freed once again from the circle of life.'

GREETINGS

Greetings from us to the lovely world,
do roses blossom in the gardens still?
Greetings to the unending sun and moon,
do lights and shadows tremble in the water?

All was lovely, snow or storm or blizzard,
day passing day,
our longing for the beating of a wing.
In the blue sky do birds still fly away?

Now we're far distant from the light,
from the child's voice, the ivy and the rose.
We've become
ships never to return.

Who now seeks after us and asks our names?

Translated by Ruth Christie

Nazım Hikmet
(1902-1963)

EXTRACTS FROM THE DIARY OF LA GIOCONDA

Paris, The Louvre, March 15, 1924

.... I'm bored in the Louvre these days.
One soon grows tired of boredom.
So now I'm bored with my boredom.
From this spiritual crisis
        I formed the opinion:
        it's fun
                to explore the Museum,
        but not to be one of its treasures.

Condemned to this palace, prison of the past,
                sentenced to grin without end,
under the oilpaint my face is beginning
        to crack with ennui
because
        I was La Gioconda of Florence
my smile better-known than my city.

I'm bored in the Louvre these days,
and since it soon gets boring talking with the past,
I
decided from now on
to keep a diary.
Perhaps writing up this day
        will help to forget the last.

The Louvre is a funny place.
Here you can find:
Alexander the Great's
        chronometric Longines watch.
But
        you can't find a common pencil

or a sheet of clean paper to write on.
Damn your Paris, your Louvre!
I'll write my memoirs
            on the back of my portrait.
Look here:
I've made a beginning
by stealing a fountain-pen
            from a short-sighted American
whose hair reeked of wine!

I'm writing on the back of my picture:
the agony of one whose smile is famous.

March 18. Night.

....
The Louvre asleep.
In the gloom the armless Venus
            resembles a World War soldier.
A Chevalier's golden helmet gleams:
the nightwatch torches light on
            an obscure painting.
Here
in the Louvre
each day is the same as another
            like the sides of a wooden cube.
My head filled with pungent smells
            like a shelf in a chemist's shop.

March 20.

....
I admire the Flemish painters.
Was it easy to give the look of a naked goddess
to the plump mistress of a sausage-merchant?
Though
            she could buy silk knickers if she liked,
a cow + silken knickers is still a cow!
Last night
            a window
                        was left open.
The naked Flemish goddesses caught cold.

All day
today
they coughed and sneezed
and turned their mountainous pink buttocks
to the crowds.
I too caught cold
I sniffed in secret from the visitors
afraid I'd be a laughing-stock
with my catarrhal smile.

April 1.

....
Today I saw a Chinese man.
Not at all in the pigtailed style of old!
And how he looked
at me!
I know very well the Chinese
exquisite carvers of ivory
don't look twice
at a stranger
....
....

April 20.

....
The papers are full of Chinese news.
I hear that now
the dragon from Kaf
the mountain surrounding the world
has spread its wings
in the golden firmament
over the Chinese homeland.
But as a result
the throat of a British lord
shaven like a plucked hen
will be cut
together with
the long
wispy
beard
of Confucius.

April 22.

....

Last night a screeching American zurna
the horn of a 12 h.p. Ford
woke me from a dream.
The moment I saw it
it vanished.

What I saw was a still blue lake!
In which the slant-eyed love of my life
had embraced a gleaming fish by the neck.
I'm going to him there
my boat a Chinese saucer,
my sail
a Japanese sunshade
of bamboo
and embroidered in silk.

May 2.

....

My Chinaman didn't come today.

May 5.

....

Nor today.

May 8.

....

My days are like
the waiting-room
of a station,
my eyes never off the tracks.

May 10.

....

Greek sculptors!
Miniature painters of Seljuk times!
Weavers of carpets of fire for Jemshid!
Readers of poetry to desert dromedaries!
Dancers like the wind!
Cutters of multi-faceted diamonds

And you
Maestro Michelangelo!
with your five skills at your fingertips
proclaim to friend and foe:
La Gioconda's beloved,
for shouting in Paris too loudly
and smashing the window
of the CHINESE
AMBASSADOR
has been evicted
from France!
My Chinese lover has gone back to China!
I wonder who they'll call
Leylâ and Mejnun* now?

May 13.

....
Today right before me
a young girl
was freshening up the lipstick
of her blood-red mouth
as my eye was caught in her mirror,
the tin crown of fame on my head fell to bits.
While the urge to cry twisted my guts
and distorted my lips,
my face grinned inanely like a roasted pig's.
If I had my way
a cubist painter could take the bones
of that Leonardo da Vinci
and make them into handles for his brushes;
for touching me with his paint-stained hands,
and sticking this cursed smile
like a gold crown in my mouth,
- it would serve him right!

(1929)

Translated by Ruth Christie.

* *Leylâ and Mejnun were the famous lovers of an eastern romance and the equivalent of Romeo and Juliet.*

POEMS FOR PIRAYÉ (HIS WIFE) FROM PRISON

20th September 1945

At this late hour
in this autumn night
I am full of your words,
eternal as time and matter,
naked as an eye,
heavy as a hand,
words clear and shining as stars.

Your words came to me,
from your heart, from your head
from your flesh.

Your words brought you:
                they are: mother,
                they are: woman,
                they are: companion.
Sorrowful, painful, joyful, hopeful,
heroic, human words.

22nd September 1945

I'm reading a book:
            you are in it.
I'm listening to a song:
            you are in it.
I sit down to eat my bread:
            you're sitting facing me.
I work:
      you're facing me.
You, who are always ready and willing:
we can't talk together,
we can't hear each other's voices:
you are my widow of eight years.

24th September 1945

The best sea: has yet to be crossed.
The best child: has yet to be born.
The best days: have yet to be lived;
and the best word that I wanted to say to you
is the word that I have not yet said.

25th September 1945

It's nine o'clock.
The bell's gone in the compound.
They'll be shutting the cell doors soon ...
This time I've been inside quite a time:
eight years.
Living is work and hope, my darling.
Living, like loving you, is serious work.

SUNDAY

It's Sunday,
today for the first time they let me out into the sun
                    and for the first time in my life
I marvelled at how far the sky was from me
                              and how vast,
                              how blue,
                              and I stood stock still.
Then I sat on the ground my good friend,
and leaned my back against the wall.

At this moment, no daydreaming,
no freedom, no wife,
just the earth, myself and the sun,
                         and happiness.

Translated by Richard McKane.

THE WALNUT TREE

My head is a foaming cloud, inside and outside I'm the sea.
I am a walnut tree in Gülhane Park in Istanbul,
an old walnut tree with knots and scars.
You don't know this and the police don't either.

I am a walnut tree in Gülhane Park,
My leaves sparkle like fish in water,
my leaves flutter like silk handkerchiefs.
Break one off, my darling, and wipe your tears.
My leaves are my hands - I have a hundred thousand hands.
Istanbul I touch you with a hundred thousand hands.
My leaves are my eyes, and I am shocked at what I see.

I look at you, Istanbul, with a hundred thousand eyes
and my leaves beat, beat with a hundred thousand hearts.
I am a walnut tree in Gulhane Park.
You don't know this and the police don't either.

(July 1, 1957)

STONE SHIP

In a park in Peking there is a ship, made of stone.
The wind fills the sails in China,
only that ship does not move,
only that ship is in trouble.

Translated by Richard McKane.

THE BRONZE SHADOW

From stone, bronze, plaster, paper
from two centimetres to seven metres
in all the city squares we were under his boots
of stone, bronze, plaster, paper
and his shadow of stone, bronze, plaster, paper
hung over the park trees.
His moustache of stone, bronze, plaster, paper
was in our soup in the restaurants
In our rooms we were under his eyes
of stone, bronze, plaster, paper
Then they disappeared
His boots disappeared from the squares
His shadow no longer hung over our trees
His moustache was no longer in our soup
His eyes departed from our rooms
and the pressure of thousands of tons
of stone, bronze, plaster, paper
was lifted off our chests.

Translated by Richard McKane.

SAD FREEDOM

You sell out - your eyes' alertness, the radiance of your hands.
You knead the dough of the bread of life, yet never taste a slice.
You are a slave working in your great freedom.
You are free,
with the freedom to suffer hell to make Croesus rich.

As soon as you're born work and worry
like windmills of lies are planted in your head.
You hold your head in your hands in your great freedom.
You are free,
in your freedom of conscience!
You are decapitated.
Your arms loll at your sides.
You wander the streets in your great freedom.
You are free,
in your great freedom of being out of work!

Wall Street grabs you by the scruff of your neck.
One day they could send you to Korea.
You could fill a pit with your great freedom.
You are free
with the freedom of being the unknown soldier.

You say you should live like a human being,
not a tool, a number, a means to an end.
They clap on the handcuffs in your great freedom.
You are free,
in your freedom to be arrested, to go into prison, even be hanged.

In your life there are no iron, bamboo or lace curtains.
There's no need to choose freedom:
you are free.
This freedom is a sad thing beneath the stars.

Translated by Richard McKane

MY FUNERAL *

Will my funeral start in our courtyard below?
How will you bring my coffin down three floors?
The lift will not take it
and the stairs are too narrow.

Perhaps the courtyard will be knee-deep in sunlight and pigeons
perhaps there will be snow and children's cries mingling in the air
or the asphalt glistening with rain
and the dustbins littering the place as usual.

If in keeping with the custom here I am to go, face open to the skies,
on the hearse, a pigeon might drop something on my brow, for luck.
Whether a band turns up or no, children will come near me,
children like funerals.

Our kitchen window will stare after me as I go,
the washing in the balcony will wave to see me off.
I have been happier here than you can ever imagine,
friends, I wish you all a long and happy life.

Moscow, April 1963

Translated by Feyyaz Kayacan Fergar

* *This was one of the last poems Nazim Hikmet wrote. He died soon afterwards.*

Ercüment Behzat Lav
(1903-84)

KUKULIKI

White, I want it white.
My house,
my garden,
my flowers,
I want them all white.

Also my night
and my heart.

THREE TIMES WHITE

The palms of our hands are white.
The soles of our feet are white.
The whites of our eyes are white.
We are three times white.
What is there left?
How much whiter can we get?

THE BIBLE AND THE LAND

When you white ones were born,
you had only the Bible to your name,
and we had the land.
Now we have the Bible
and you have the land.

THE BASE OF THE PYRAMID

We are the base of the pyramid,
you are on top, we are below.
You live up there with the angels
thick as thieves.
This is as it should be.

I TOO CAN DIE OF LOVE

Oh my white master
I too can burn
finer than white.
I too,
I too,
can die of love

Translated by Feyyaz Kayacan Fergar

Necip Fazıl
(1905-83)

POET

I am the poet, prying locksmith of invisible things
I am the angel of inquisition, steering life's funerals

DEPTHLESS WELL

cold segments of worms on my mouth
        sands will haunt my eyes
I shall sleep as long as a depthless well

PRAY

you thrust a dagger in my shadow
my warm blood spreads all over
come and see my country
come and see my headless people

shed tears to bring in the tide
maybe the ship will be salvaged

STRENGTH

do not tap against the window I may jump out of my skin
do not touch me, my flesh may slide into emptiness

Translated by Mevlut Ceylan

RAILWAY STATION

this is the place where man
is sucked into the silt of tedious days
suddenly a bell rings
darker than tolling death

then a whistle screams
stating in stuttering bursts:
'they leave with familiar faces today,
tomorrow they'll return as stark strangers'

UNAWARE

if only I could stop this passer-by
if only I could tell him
to treasure his few remaining steps

HIDDEN

do not touch me, do not disturb
this madness in me
do not torture secrets that can't see me

Translated by Feyyaz Kayacan Fergar

Cahit Sıtkı Tarancı
(1910-56)

THE TRAIN

We died hoping so much from death.
In a vast emptiness the magic was broken.
How can you not remember that song,
a handful of sky, a bundle of twigs, bird feathers.
Living was something we had grown used to.
There's no news from that world now.
There's no one to call on us, no one to miss us.
No window can dispel the depths of our night.
Running waters no longer carry our image.

MORNING PRAYER

Beautiful day, lovely light,
take your time coming into the world.
In you are the mountains majestic,
in you are the plains endless.

I am grateful that I can count
the chimney stacks of my town.
My dear mother's prayer was for every
chimney to have its own smoke.

Look at the merry trees
leaf by leaf shimmering.
Look at the happy flight of these birds,
feel my heart beating in their wings.

Translated by Feyyaz Kayacan Fergar

Fazıl Hüsnü Dağlarca
(b. 1914)

THE SINGLE LEAF

Leave me alone with the seasons
you animals, you caves.
But what is it that calls me
in the wake of waters and after the trees?

It is not in the forest, not in the air,
it is not in the eye, not in the head.
It is further than the dark of night
yet smaller.

Like a single leaf
it covers earth and sky.
Motionless, it warmly dwells
on hand, face and fate.

THE GOOD DEATH

When you died,
they buried you in the earth,
they buried you in the stones.

The green of the grass,
the sleep of the insects
took place in your heart.

A tuft of moss, a pebble,
a root, moved aside a bit,
made room for you.

In all this
you were buried.

Translated by Feyyaz Kayacan Fergar

THREE POEMS FROM THE LEGEND OF CHAKIR

1

All the things that are in me and outside of me
become evident with the coming of the dark.
It is a probing surge against the world
in the shape of hand, foot and thought.

An oleander flowering across the years
sways from wind to wind.
Was the midwife who delivered me
beautiful? I still want to know.

2

I'm not alone, there's the tree too.
It bears fruit, it bears birds,
it thinks along the branches of my words
with the wind playing on its lips.

All mountains have a share
in the vast domain of my being.
It is so easy, so near;
thoughts look like breathing.

I'm not alone, there's the water,
there's the insect too, followed
by nights and days and always there is
a lovely face turning somewhere towards me.

3

Mountains rise
prosperous and tall.
The stars, our lords in the sky,
stand over the majesty of prestigious nights
in dreams of timelessness.

And I? What do I do?
Who says I must stay in my little house,
who says I must sit at my little table,
beside the jug and the lamp -
who says all that?

QUESTION

Who will take me to his garden
cool with willows and coy water?
When my body, painless, shines from the dark,
I shall ask: whose is the garden?

A thick sleep will be cast in my eyes,
I'll gather good marks for good behaviour;
floating aslant within a strange sea,
I shall ask: who sleeps this sleep?

They'll take away my face, my arms, my neck;
in a place where life runs deep,
on the last rung of my straining ghost,
I shall ask: who dies this death?

Translated by Feyyaz Kayacan Fergar

THE MARKETPLACE

This marketplace frightens me.
        There are people in it
        some ugly, some fair.
I take the pulse of their breaths
as if I had risen from their beds.

They shape stones into man,
        man into earth;
They pretend not to know,
self is pretence's monolith.

Cabs, trams, street vendors pass by
        I fall asleep a little.
People scatter toward the squares,
        my sorrow stays put.

WARNING

I want my heart to shine
before it is driven into blankness,
I want the green to open the light.
Earth, let me walk in your warning.

What are, after all, Time's archaeologies?
        Walking life after life after life,
        I walked generations adding up
to less than the feeble height of an oat.

Translated by Feyyaz Kayacan Fergar

HANGED

He is hanged in the middle of the square as dawn breaks,
anguish fills the squares.
Not a plum tree, not a rosebush,
on earth this daybreak there is a single voice, the gallows tree.

Hanged bright white on blue,
as if he talks, eats, drinks,
sways as though he's walking towards the past,
a journey even to the first men.

Hanged, his arms inside his shirt,
without waving his hand to anybody.
He's walked far, he's travelled far in this world,
evident from the patch on his shoe.

Perhaps hanged to the skies, to the skies,
perhaps his life is shorter than an insect's.
Not naked
he can't be counted as dead.

Hanged as he thought something else,
his mind distant from all points of the compass,
he sways,
a lily in bygone lands.

He heard the decision of the court and was hanged.
His understanding shines in his eyes.
He sways, leaf on leaf
the crimes on our body.

Hanged without shame and without fear,
face wide open, his chest turned towards us,
can you hear
his marching song?

Translated by Richard McKane

HOPE

Here
I believe.
There
the bird flies.

IN MARRIAGE

When women get married
they blend
into the endless
widowhood of waiting.

THE POWER OF WHITE

As loaves diminish
our hands
grow.

HUGE

Farmers' hands
grow in the soil,
birds' eyes
grow in the sky.

Translated by Talat S. Halman

GUILT-DRIVEN MADNESS
(from the Hiroshima poems)

I am the driver of this heavenly chariot
but the almighty blue has no say in my head;
in the turmoil of the last stars
my hands are caught in the imminence of fate.

I steered this plane from a myriad past to a myriad year.
What folly shall hurtle out of my wits?
The doors of an era unfolded and bare-footed
I noiselessly seemed to cross paths of light.

I pulled the bomb lever
and Hiroshima, the flower, petalled off into extinction.
How can it be? Where did I gather these multiples of death?
My mind becomes a fire-bird and erupts into dark, dark flights.

WHAT THE CHILDREN SAID
(from the Hiroshima poems)

Eiko said: half the mothers and fathers are dead,
what shall the children do now?
This bomb spells the end of children.

Shintara said: half the students are dead,
what shall the mothers and fathers do now?
This bomb spells the end of mothers and fathers.

Kenyi said: they are all dead now, mothers, fathers and children.
Had we not prayed towards the sky last night?
This bomb spells the end of God.

Translated by Feyyas Kayacan Fergar

*ITAI**
(from the Hiroshima poems)

The widow of the tailor came out of the ruins,
life cannot be committed to earth.
Her smallest child is up to his neck caught in the rubble.
Like a wounded tigress she charges, hands
transmuted into spades, into pickaxes.
Life cannot be committed to earth.

Two crimson screams, one within the other,
life cannot be committed to earth.
Oh, hear the other orphaned voices:
"Save us from the darkness of death."
Life cannot be committed to earth.

Living is as holy as the sky is blue,
it cannot be committed to earth.
- *Itai!* Oh my love, how it must hurt.
Life cannot be committed to earth

Translated by Feyyas Kayacan Fergar

* *Itai (pronounced it-a-i) means "it hurts" in Japanese.*

Orhan Veli
(1914-50)

RAG AND BONE MAN

I buy rags and bones,
I buy them and turn them into stars.
Music is the food of the soul:
I rave, rave about music.

I write poems,
I write them to buy
rags and bones.
I sell them back
to buy songs and tunes.

But I wish, I wish
I was a fish
in a bottle of raki.

Translated by Feyyaz Kayacan Fergar

OUTSIDE THE TOWN

The buds that are just bursting
promise good days.
And a woman outside the town
on the grass,
under the sun,
stretched out face down,
on her breasts and belly
feels the sun.

Translated by Richard McKane.

LETTERS TO OKTAY

I

Freezing cold winter.
I write you my first letter
in the Hungarian restaurant.
Oktay, my friend,
tonight all the drinkers
send you greetings.

II

It's raining outside now,
clouds pass by in the mirror,
and these days Melih and I
are in love with the same girl.

III

I've been looking for a job for a month,
without a penny, my clothes in rags.
If I did not love her
perhaps I would not wait
for the day when I will die for men.

Translated by Richard McKane.

IN

We have seas in the sun.
We have trees in the leaf.
Morning till evening
between our seas and trees
we come and go in rags.

Translated by Feyyaz Kayacan Fergar

I ACCUSE
(The Butcher's Cat to the Alley Cat)

You keep saying you're hungry
that shows you are a communist
that proves you were the one
who set fire to all those houses,
the ones in Istanbul
and the ones in Ankara as well.
What a vile beast you are!

MORO ROMANTICO

If I cried could you see
the voice in my verse?
Could you with your hands
touch my tears?

I did not know songs could be so lovely
and words so short
until I fell under this spell.

There is a place, I know,
where language tells.
Sometimes I feel I am almost there,
but I cannot put it into words.

Translated by Feyyaz Kayacan Fergar

LEFT HAND

I got drunk
and remembered you again
my left hand,
my poor, clumsy left hand.

MY SHADOW

I am bored to extinction
having year in year out
dragged him behind my heels.
Why can we not live a little
he in his own privacy
I in my own?

FREE

Everything in life is free, free.
The air is free, clouds are free,
hills and dales are free,
free the rain and the mud ...

Window-shopping is free,
looking at cars is free.
Hands off the bread and the cheese,
but help yourself to brackish water.

Freedom is a price on your head.
Slavery costs nothing.
Everything in life is free.

Translated by Feyyaz Kayacan Fergar

APRIL

It is impossible
to write poems
if you are in love.
It is impossible
not to write them
if April is the month.

NEAR DEATH

Towards evening in winter time
a sick man stands at his window.
I am not the only one who feels alone.
The sea is dark, the sky is dark,
the birds look strange.

Forget that I am poor, that I am lonely
towards evening in winter time.
I too have had my go at love affairs,
fame, women, money.
With the passing of time eyes are unlocked.
Is it the thought of death that makes us sad?
In this ellipse of life what have we done
what have we seen
except evil things?

When we die, we too become clean,
when we die, we too become good men.
Fame, women, money
we forget all.

Translated by Feyyaz Kayacan Fergar

Oktay Rifat
(1914-88)

FATE

What a sad fate mine is!
I have no head for figures
and here I am working as an accountant.
I love aubergine dishes,
they don't agree with me.
I know a freckle-faced girl,
I love her.
She doesn't love me.

Translated by Feyyaz Kayacan Fergar

TO MY WIFE

You bring coolness to the halls,
a sense of space to rooms.
To wake in your bed in the morning
gives me daylong joy.

We are two halves of the apple,
our day and night
our house and home are one.
Happiness is a meadow,
where you tread
it springs to life.
Loneliness comes from the road you go down.

Translated by Ruth Christie

LAMENT

First your outer covering wore away,
Your flesh, your eyes and eyebrows wore away,
Whatever you knew as fresh and young, burned out,
burned out.

Hand and foot you lost my friend,
Pen-slim finger and nail.
Life and spirit once were yours,
now lost and gone,
What's left of you, my friend, reduced
to lines in books.
- Where lashes, hair and skin?

O shoddy world!
- But once an Orhan Veli lived.
Come, brother Orhan, come,
Take my hands,
Use my eyes.

Translated by Ruth Christie

PADISHAH

Selim the First loved blood
Selim the Second - wine
Selim the Third - music and poetry
Selim the Fourth never existed -
thank God.

Translated by Richard McKane

FREEDOM HAS HANDS

1

Our horses galloped foaming
to the calm sea.

2

What is this flight? Is it the dove's
joy of freedom?

3

It was forbidden to kiss, did you know,
forbidden to think,
forbidden to defend the work force.

4

They've picked the fruit from the tree
and they sell it in the market
for as much as they can get,
labour's broken branches on the ground.

5

Light is blinding, they say,
and freedom is explosive.
Arsonists smash our lamps
and with oily rags set fire to freedom.

As soon as we reach out, they want an explosion,
and they want us to catch fire when we light the flame.
There are mine-fields,
bread and water wait in the darkness.

6

Freedom has hands,
eyes, feet;
to wipe the bloody sweat,
to look at tomorrows,
heading straight for equality.

7

I'm the cage, you are the ivy;
tangle, tangle as much as you are able!

8

Love of freedom is this:
once you're tempted there's no escape,
it's a habit that never gets old,
a dream that is truer than reality.

9

The historic flow of brave herdsmen,
the workers, bees of the universe's beehive;
milling round black bread,
brothers who bring freedom to our world.
By that bread the mind is roused from sleep,
our endless night dawns with that bread;
people attain independence with that sun.

10

This hope is the door to freedom,
half open to happy days.
This joy is the light of happy days,
gently, timidly its rays strike us.

Come people of my land, show yourselves
like a budding branch at the door of freedom,
and behind you the sky is brotherly blue.

Translated by Richard McKane

HE

He enters by door and window together,
he brings me gifts,
he's both at the head and the foot of my bed,
and under my bed and in it.

Who is he? Whom does he ask for?
What news does he want to give?
How will he tell his trouble?
Where are his lips? Where are his hands?

He sits in every armchair at once,
aimless he wanders,
he thinks my room is his,
he drinks my water and reads my books.

But in my dreams,
he shows me curious pictures from afar,
trees, mountains, houses, more
and oh - much more!

Translated by Ruth Christie

FLAME

In the morning of adventures outgrown
chestnut trees resume my childhood.
The candle-flame touches
birds bygone and quivers.

Translated by Feyyaz Kayacan Fergar

THE STONES

All night long in my tightly folded hands
I must have kept my shivering stones.
Waking in the morning I saw them standing:
the pigeon on the eaves, the cat on the threshold,
the cloud on the roofs.
My loneliness was ashore in the mirror.
Waking in the morning I saw it standing
over sun and tree.

GIRLS

Girls are green and sometimes blue,
they point toward the sky the streets
of our towns. Girls are our sailing clouds
we look at, crouched at the bottom of walls.
Without thinking we think of a port, we make
our way through trees, there comes the sound of the sea,
a pomegranate shows us her breasts.
Through the door half-open
we see in the house
the staircase helping up a lovely carpet.

Girls are green and sometimes blue.

Translated by Feyyaz Kayacan Fergar

EARTH

I stepped on the wet earth. Suddenly
        I was a tree, I was bud, I was knot.
                Toward the sun I turned
my leaf-drawn face. I heard that breeze
        in the headlong sky. Come close,
lovely girls, come close and with linked hands
        dance in circles around me.

IN MY SLEEP

I found it in my sleep. It was
standing in the green of the grass.
Scant and sad, like the face of a child,
small endlessly,
it was looking at a bygone part of me;
a swallow softly brushing it
flew over, singing.
Oh I loved it so, tears singing in my eyes.

Then, like the others, it disappeared.

Translated by Feyyaz Kayacan Fergar

IN THE STREET

In the street narrowing like a cat's eye
the rain's slippery rope over my shoulder
I walk towing an old funeral after me.

I move within the axis of my own image
I open a door that looks like me.
One of my eyes has fallen asleep.
The other one is still up.

The night like a scorpion keeps
crawling down the wall.

Translated by Feyyaz Kayacan Fergar

TREE ANECDOTE

That year the cherry blossoms of the spring
instead of staying to fruit
were dropping off untimely.
The garden was deserted,
I was not there, nor you,
and these lines perhaps had not yet been written.

A horseman came from the South,
he looked at the blossoms on the ground,
he hung his whip on the tree,
he turned his horse's head and went.

Translated by Ruth Christie

Melih Cevdet Anday
(b. 1915)

THE MAP OF HEAVEN

Listen to me, my immortal soul,
when I die, remember not to go
winging your way up to Heaven.
The Big Bear is there, and the Little Bear,
the Scorpion, the Snake, the centipede,
the ox, the bull,
they are all up there.

Stay put, my soul,
Heaven is no place for you.

LETTER FROM A DEAD FRIEND

I live as before
taking walks, thinking...
except that without a ticket
I can now get on a boat or train.
My buying and selling I do
without the need to bargain.
I am at home all nights, I am at ease,
if only I could open the window when bored,
or scratch my head, pick flowers
and every now and then shake the hand of a friend.

LYRICISM

Lyricism before and beyond everything,
before matter, history, B.C.
before your left before your right,
lyricism on an empty belly.

Lyricism is the apple of the eye,
lyricism is common sense,
lyricism is a lobster
or a tin of baked beans.

What a divine thing lyricism is:
some wear it to keep warm,
others as a feather in their cap,
oh I adore lyricism.

We see in this soup the presence
of most of its ingredients,
salt, pepper, oil for instance,
yes, but what about lyricism?

Lyricism is the East End,
lyricism is the Prince's Islands,
lyricism water-cheap,
lyricism the lion's share.

NO REMEDY

I understand, there is no remedy
against death, ill-fate, accidents;
there is no cure for baldness,
I grant you all that.
But what about unemployment,
what about going hungry,
Do they also brook no remedy?
This I do not understand.

THE ORDERLY WORLD

I do so love this orderly world
with its winters and summers
its springs and autumns
its nights and days neatly in a row.

Trees are rooted in earth
therefore all trees must be rooted in earth
Mountains rise head up
therefore all mountains must rise head up
People are reasonable
therefore all people must be reasonable.
The five fingers are where they belong
the thumb, the fore, the middle, the third and the little fingers.
Can you imagine the little finger daring to move
towards the middle one? Perish the thought!
Suppose an acacia tree takes a stroll
head deep in earth
exchanging greetings with chestnut and pine:
Peace be with you, who are you, what are you, where are you?
Imagine the roots of the acacia becoming the topic of the day
the wind would have a howling fit...
Oh dear, oh dear, its roots are in the air, are in the air...
Come on, what harm is there if a big mountain
is turned upside down...
Oh God, oh Heaven forbid
I do so love this orderly world...
the dead well below
the quick well above
let's enjoy this double-tiered euphoria.

THE LAUREL WOOD

Slave-owners who never went short of bread
were free to dabble in philosophy
for their slaves were there to provide the bread.
Never worried about bread, the slaves
never dabbled in philosophy, for their masters
were there to secure the bread.
This was the way to Lycia's decline and fall.

Slaves unworried by philosophy
went on making bread, for it was
from their masters that they received philosophy.
The makers of philosophy who were never short of slaves
did not make bread, for philosophy
was there, to provide the slaves.
This was the way to Lycia's decline and fall.

So philosophy had no bread, bread
no philosophy. The philosophy of derelict bread
was bred on the bread of derelict philosophy
and the derelict bread of philosophy
was bred on the derelict philosophy of bread.
This was the way to Lycia's decline and fall
but it still lies under a green laurel wood.

Extract from "ODYSSEUS BOUND"

I

You my senses my ancient trees
devouring each night all your birds,
you my motley feast of lanterns,
and you the derelict games
of my blindbuffing days,
in the ceaseless renewal
of your dark obstinacy,
you keep laying and clearing this table.

II

My loneliness thronged about me
as I ran haywire in a skidding world.
I looked at myself through a dinothorium's eye,
- what madness - in a gull's beak
alien and remote the sea was dangling uprooted.
Feather by slow feather the wind became a bird,
a little later the thunder was a tree.

III

It was bound to come to this,
I dealt so much in feelings.
There is no secret, no trust,
faith or rhyme left between us.
In the end I used up my soul.
When I rejoice I observe myself rejoicing,
when I am afraid, it is not with my fear.
Since the door is standing ajar
open it extremely.
I am free now of the man in me,
and I shall live love lovelessly.

Translated by Feyyaz Kayacan Fergar

Müştak Erenus
(b. 1915)

DUTY BOUND

As an honourable citizen of this world
I shall prop my ladder against the clouds
and release this carrier-pigeon
straight into the skies
in the name of God and all his attributes
in the name of the love of man.

I shall report you all...
what have you done to this world?

A CARNATION FOR THE SUN

I get up in the morning
I stick a carnation behind the sun's ear
a lively red carnation
to celebrate in style the beginning of a new day.
Look at the sun now so handsome
with shining cockiness
with bright bravura.
Oh the swank and the swagger.
Hats off here comes the dandy sun.

THIS WAY TO THE WAR PLEASE

When a fight is on birds forget to fly
turn to stone and fall to the ground.
But what can you find to say to these men
in this soul-gouging war?
Forgetting this sky, this sun
they choose the road to effluents of death.

Translated by Feyyaz Kayacan Fergar

İlhan Berk
(b. 1916)

PABLO PICASSO

L'Homme au Mouton
A lonely cloud, a lonely branch, a light,
the sky, the flower, the water's feeling of nothing to follow, of love,
yearning and joy,
a little hope, a little ray, the morning a little further on,
different one by one, differently beautiful, differently lonely
and near,
all these worldly things drifted by uselessly.

Picasso picked up his brush.

Nature morte
Picasso woke up
into his sunburnt hands.

THE SUN

The sun rises with its water-colour kit,
sits on the roof.
Renews itself.

WOODCOCK

I am September, who are you,
said the laurel.
The woodcock distilled himself
into flight.

I am looking for the voice.

SUMMER

Summer comes out of the door
for a stroll. Timid on the threshold
takes off its clothes
to enter this poem.

PICTURE

Two horses graze
in the dry grass.
A woman hangs up her washing.
Unknowing they magnify the plain.

ARRIVAL

I left death threadbare
I am on my way

A VISIT TO THE WIFE OF A DEAD POET

"Papers, books," she said, "wherever I put my hand.
Here, a half of a poem, but here one that has been miraculously
made whole. Everything comes to life in poetry, isn't it true?
It is in a poem that a dawn takes place. It is in poems
that streets come and go.
This was the way we lived."

Her voice,
as if coming from long long ago
roamed through broken, silent rooms.
She then showed a book lying open on the table.
The last one his hand was to touch.
"He was seated here reading this book.
We saw it slip through his fingers and fall."

She spoke no more. She covered her face with her hands,
as if distressed by a moving cloud.

QUESTION

Tulip, how are you?
Where are you off to like that?

THE ART OF LOVE

He loved making love to trees.

He grew up
in and out of my bed.

Translated by Feyyaz Kayacan Fergar

Behçet Necatigil
(1916-79)

REASONS

Reasons for getting angry
proliferate as we grow old.
We remember, we regret
the raw mistakes of youth.

We live a bit longer for the sake
of a lovely poem, a telling story.
Looking back, the scales are loaded
in favour of our youth.

We used to count the days -
now we have run out of them

UNTITLED

I have sat too long with you
can I get up and go?
Even if I were to
I'd still be with you.

What were the books
what were the tongues
they searched us in?
Statistics are important.

If you're going to be alone
I'll stay.
We pulled ourselves back.
This was what we wanted.

FOREWORD

Once there was a Behçet Necatigil,
who lived his dreams.
In the middle of the night
in the middle of the street
he would put things on paper.
A poet - he left us
these windmills as memories.

HOUSESCAPE

The room lacks nothing,
buffet table, mirror, carpets.
The fire was on when I got home.

They had filled the carafe of water for me,
my bed was made from the night before.
Soft light falls
from the table-lamp.

A couple of stars in the sky.
The landlady left me
sitting all by myself.
Items of furniture have voices of their own.
Loneliness belongs to God alone.

The room lacks nothing.
The town is asleep.
I should have a wife, a child
in this setting, in this housescape.

VISIT ON A FEAST DAY

He had no place
no one to visit

so he went to see
the lions in the park.
The lions are of stone
and he a man.

How could they get on?

They did.

AIR

The chimney smoke mixes with the air.
I thought of you just now, felt exhausted.

Scores of youngsters out there play around with love.
They're so absorbed, if their mothers were to call
'Come in dinner is ready' they would all feel undone.

He will run for a long time yet to breast the tape.
Who else is racing, I thought of you just now.

THE WAGER

It looks like
our wager will take some time.

Leaving work and occupation
I moved to a house facing the cemetery.

Death you cannot cheat me
the wager is still on.

THE CLOSE LAMENT

This is awkward, a quick solution must be found.
If the doctor is dead, how sad to see
his brass plaque hanging on the door
of the house.

How many mountains did I cross to get here?
I have no strength for distances -
I can't see how they could have
rubbed me off their eyes.

One should divide the brief joy into days,
into flowers that fade twice.
What if a bird were to fall in this heat?

THE WALL

He was thrown against a wall and fell to pieces,
he can go nowhere now without putting himself together,
too many things were too late realised.

Consolation is an art but not within articulate reach,
timetables rot inside my pockets.

We are all exiles in islands of pity;
a chunk of life gets spent anyway,
whether we join processions or not.

Translated by Feyyaz Kayacan Fergar

Cahit Külebi
(b. 1917)

THE EAST

There were hundreds and thousands of lice
crawling on the bedsheets, on the clothes,
some were spreading out thin, others moved
in thick, serried ranks.

This is the East. Lice, earthquake, sorrow.
What you call happiness is a thin slice of bread,
what you call happiness is a handful of coal,
the rest is snow, mud and dried dung. (*)

A black blood flows through the nights,
death flows also and helplessness.
The dawn light, the sound of barking dogs,
the crowing of cocks rise like dust.

This is the East. A backward, taciturn, bitter country.
What you call a rose is a field flower there,
what you call fruit grow in the wild there.
In the end, all you get from the hand of the beloved
is the elixir of fate.

This is the East. People there look at you
with the eyes of a dead sheep's head.
Love, warmth, softness have been
for a thousand years left behind in the folksongs.

* *dried dung is used as a fuel in the East, i.e. the easternmost regions of Anatolia.*

PASSING

My bright days deserted me,
to be left behind is sad!

It is sad to be haunted by songs,
haunted by the smell of meadows!

An airplane hangs up in the sky,
to take off and not to go is sad!

Is it God, is it friend or foe,
finding out brings much sorrow!

Our spell in this world is so brief,
thinking of it brings much sorrow.

Translated by Feyyaz Kayacan Fergar

Salah Birsel
(b.1919)

I TOO STOOD UP

I too stood up under this sky.
I too wrote poetry
and learned a thing or two about emotions.

But nobody could see
I had something to say,
nobody lent an ear
to the love in my heart.

Oh, the time has come and gone,
loneliness is my better half.

FOURSOME REEL

Mr Dumburbeyli, an illustrious poet,
copiously detests Mr Bumburbeyli.
Mr Bumburbeyli, another poet of fame,
looks down his non-stop nose at Mr Dumburbeyli.

For Lumburbeyli, a poet of substance,
Mr Dumburbeyli and Mr Bumburbeyli are
of no consequence. Mr Jumburbeyli, another poet
of note, feels only disgust for Mr Lumburbeyli.

Mr Dumbur and Mr Bumburbeyli
shower insult and abuse on Mr Lumbur and Mr Jumburbeyli.

From the sequence "HAYDAR HAYDAR"

XIII

Your dark eyes are caught
like a writing in my throat.
Wait a bit, wait,
let me count the doves.

XXXI

I have been kicked out of every poem
down endless roads,
on a par with every dog.

Translated by Feyyaz Kayacan Fergar

Feyyaz Kayacan Fergar
(b. 1919)

THE WINDOW

For Miroslav Holub

Let us start with small things,
let us into the memory of the palm of our hand
draw a window.
Let us open it: to let things in.
For instance
the cool shade of a small tree,
for instance
a fish just in time for the sea,
for instance
the sum of a seed,
a look that serves a purpose,
a child who stands on the tip of our tongue,
the eye of a needle that bewitches an embroidery.

Even if nothing comes in
let us open the window.
We will have had at least
a bit of fresh air,
a bit of hope.

Is that bad?

THE MEMORY MAN

Should a single thread
of sun or living time
seep into his room,
it would turn to evil eye
embossed on the walls.

Memories tattooed on threadbare skin,
this man holds his breath
in moth-laden hands.
He inhales past gardens, past houses,
rehearses the flight of cancelled swallows
and spells a wheel to spin
the speech of unseeing.

Hanging in a corner of his voice
he compiles his own dissolution.
With driftwood-fingers, he counts
the strokes of his waxen soul.
Look by look his eyes
will ebb away and turning to stone
achieve the last inward flourish of sclerosis.

QUESTIONS

How are you? We are happy.
What time is it? We are happy.
Are you moss? We are happy.
Are you dregs? We are happy.

Is your scalp good for soup making? We are happy.
How many times a day do you agonise? We are happy.

Are you a window at the bottom
of a
well? We are happy.

Can you give me your hand? We are happy.
Where is your hand? We are happy.

Extract from "GATHERING THE DATA"

This is the question that now
urgently stands:

Shall the sum of our steps
amount to a pinch of ashes

or
shall it voice the surging strength
of a road?

This is the brunt
and the hub of the matter.
The rest is gossip or philosophy

LAMENT OF THE MISLED

Into our hands they hurriedly shoved
crumpled maps drawn by itinerant deadends.

And they said to us with embossed voices
"Go now, we wish you a safe, a clear
journey.
Go far, go well, all horizons are legible."

This send-off was a recidivist rite
acted out with eye-catching gusto.

As a generous footnote to their gesture
we heard them calling to us from afar
-- who was moving, who motionless? --
"We have done our utter best, the rest
is up to you in all directions.
Steer a probing course, keep
a good head on your shoulders."
Easier said than done!
Our eyes seemed to have been lured away
and our heads,
they are nowhere, nowhere to be found.

Translated by the author

Sabahattin Kudret Aksal
(b. 1920)

From the sequence "GUESTS"

The sky goes off its grooves
to release its birds
and then returns to where it had been.

The crowing of a snail announces
the arrival of a new day. The morning was
made up of white hulls entirely
alive in sleep
but gone on waking up,
something went missing on a rising scale.

WORDS

It is words that hold the mind together
it is words again that come to undo it.

MEMENTO MORI

He died
we buried him
his first rain fell tonight.

BOOK

One day in a curdled summer I came across a book in a box-room. It was an old book, with torn covers, loose, tattered pages turning yellowish brown. When had it been printed? No way of telling. Yet even then somehow, though it looked old, I could feel stirrings creeping through it. Back over from more than a century, a voice would call on me. The far now had become the near with it: I turned this way, that way, looked for a title. Couldn't find any. I thought of one and now I am putting it in its place:

INSIDE THE DEAD ONE'S MOUTH

Translated by Feyyaz Kayacan Fergar

Necati Cumalı
(b. 1921)

LOVELY LIGHT

You shine in bright, sweet beauty
to sustain in my eyes
the blue of the sky, the spray of the sea,
the flowering of lemons.
It was in your eye that I kissed my girl.

You etch into being my white-washed room,
the face of my mother, our table,
and the dreams youth is fond of.
It is of you I think
when despair prowls about.

We were poor people,
but our hearts were true.
You stood by us in times of plenty
or in darkest season.
You always shine in bright, sweet beauty.

Translated by Feyyaz Kayacan Fergar

A SMALL PLACE IN THE PROVINCES

A strange fear hovers
over the faces I recall.
Whenever I think of them
at the marketplace or at the café
those faces darken like a well.

The men there always look haggard.
They toil but earn little, they seldom talk,
their hearts bulge with anger.
At the slightest doubt they strike their wives
and lying in ambush they shoot a man.

The people I used to know there
gazed at the sky with fear
gazed at the sea with fear
and trembled at the sight of the landlord
scared of God scared of death
scared of the gendarmerie
scared of all government officials.

Translated by Talat S. Halman

Özdemir Asaf
(1923-81)

JURY

All colours grew dirty at the same rate:
white was given the winning prize.

APOPHTHEGM

He came into the world, they cried for joy.
He left the world, they cried bitterly.

He had lived in between:
this never occurred to them.

ARMLESS

I throw many many knives in my dreams:
they all find their target

POEM

Ships pass by as if playing a little joke.
Who can tell if they are coming or going
who can tell if birds are flying or falling?
And they who mutter falling down and getting up
who can tell if they are dying
or living?

ADVENTURE

When I began to walk on the seas
those running on land stopped to look at me
I therefore went to sink one by one
the islands I could have taken refuge in.

Translated by Feyyaz Kayacan Fergar

Arif Damar
(b. 1925)

THE RAVEN

This raven must be a fool.
One after the other
he cawed three times
and the early morning silence
was ruined.

Black now, oh
so tar-black

and now he flies out
towards the waves
in the wake of seagulls.
Will you look now ...

This raven must be
out of his foolish mind.

FLOWERPOT

A little while ago
there was a little flowerpot
in my hand, an empty flowerpot.

How was I to know it was so heavy,
oh how my arm aches.
A little while ago
there was an empty
a very empty
flowerless flowerpot.

HEAVY

There is something heavy over there
very heavy on the voice.

Over there there is something heavy
very heavy on the eye.

Here, there and here again
there is something heavy
which weighs and weighs and squats
on the lips of every word.

IN THE NAME OF LIFE

Heroism, in fact, is -
awareness of love,
it is work
done by many or by one,
finer than the power that moves
flowers and as deep as motherhood.

You'll have to stand fast.
You'll have to impeach death.

For the sake of life
in the name of life.

Translated by Feyyaz Kayacan Fergar

Attila İlhan
(b. 1925)

THE FINE ROVER

Get out of my way boy.
I won't stay still even if they tie me down.
Get me my metal staff, my iron-shod sandals.
What can I do?
Time to hit the road.
Evening perches again on the trees with the crows.
The wind beats it from place to place.
The fallen broken stars shine in the distance.
The radio waves run after me.
I was born a traveller.
The Sun Mountain roads pass through my heart.
Lines are like grape clusters ripening inside me.
The raindrops are on my lips.
The roads take me off:
I was born a traveller.
I was the rivers meeting the seas.
I said evening.
This great world I said.
To cry I said.
Once you take to the road it's for life,
searching for lunch and wine,
following the cranes,
deserting great cities, great loves
in tears and sadness.
I have loved like a child, have suffered like a giant.
All the worlds are in my veins,
despite wars, starvation, loneliness.
I was born a traveller,
what can I do?
I said there's a fairy land.
Homeland I said.
I said freedom.

Translated by Richard McKane.

LA DONNA E MOBILE

It is the end of the year 1951. I live
in the company of a rain Paris alone can design.
The streets belong to me, I belong to the streets,
a song looks for the tip of my tongue.

I'm stopping at rue de Maubeuge.
The hotel register says 'poet'.
My neighbour is a student at the Conservatoire,
every morning at ten he vocalises
with the Duke's aria from Rigoletto.

The fellow has a pure sky-blue voice.
Singing is another way of life,
we all host songs in our hearts.
This is the song of our deeds
through our second year at college.

Of course I keep thinking of my brother.
You don't know him. He may walk like an exclamation
mark but he always lights an elegant cigarette.
I am lonely now, he more than me
to the right and to the left of Rigoletto.

This boy carries the world in his heart,
the heart is a good place for the world.
One New Year's night, nose-diving drunk,
my brother pulled the skirt of la donna
in a crowded thoroughfare of Istanbul.

The wayfarer, the man of many songs,
has a tune for every wind and corner.
The rain is back on Boulevard Sébastopol,
the sun is bright over Belleville.
But la donna disappears down the Métro at Barbès.

Translated by Feyyaz Kayacan Fergar

Ahmet Arif
(1926-91)

YOUR LOVE NEVER LEFT ME

Your love never left me.
I hungered and thirsted
in the treacherous, dark night.
My soul was a stranger, my soul was silent,
my soul was shattered ...
And my hands were handcuffed,
I was without tobacco or sleep,
but your love never left me ...

Translated by Richard McKane

Can Yücel
(b. 1926)

PINS

My mother was in love with my father,
and he with her.
Let's take a walk on Wednesday, said my father.
My mother from outside the city, had no chic clothes,
and asked to borrow her sister's wedding dress.
My aunt being fatter, her dress didn't fit my mother,
so they fixed it together on her with basting and pins.
My father came, as arranged, to the house beyond Topkapi,
collected my mother and after several tram-rides
brought his Aphrodite to Bebek.
There they walked on the hills behind.
My father set down my mother in the meadow
and showed her the sea.
They talked of pleasant matters.
He was just about to kiss my mother,
and she had long been willing,
when casting his hand here and there
didn't those pins in the dress stick in his hand!
Ah! shouted my father —
Because of that day in that meadow, that moment
when I fell into my mother's imagination,
my manner of talking
both in poetry and life
is like that - full of pins.

Translated by Ruth Christie

MAN'S PRINCIPAL LAW

This is man's law of the blood:
to make wine from the grape
to strike fire from the stone
and human beings from kisses!

This is man's law of the soul:
no matter what happens to live
in the face of poverty and wars
and a thousand and one calamities!

This is man's law of reason:
to convert water to light
to render the dream true
to make the enemy a friend!

This is man's principal law
from the child on all fours
to the runner in space
to be always on course!

Translated by Ruth Christie

POEM 2

Tomorrow is Sunday, no one is allowed out.
It is census day, the national head-count day.

Well, so what! We'll stay indoors
tomorrow as well. That's not the end of the world.

Translated by Feyyaz Kayacan Fergar

METAMORPHOSIS

The long lithe creature
was dashing itself
again
and again on the stones.
Was it fed up
or was it dying in pain?
'No sir,' said the man nearby
'The snake is changing its shirt.
From this behaviour we understand more or less
that we too at one time
are thought to have changed our form.'

Translated by Ruth Christie

CASTING NET

A dripping sky came up with the nets,
the fishermen were blue all over.

Translated by Feyyaz Kayacan Fergar

THE LATEST SITUATION IN CHILE

People got so used to saying indoors
that curfews were declared illegal.

Translated by Feyyaz Kayacan Fergar

LAST WORD

With my own hands I closed
my earthly eyes.
It was worth the tiring effort.
Only death was left. It too I have now seen
feeling glad that I had been born.

POEM 26

We can show you two kinds of people
who've learned a thing or two about political finesse:
politicians and convicts.
The reason is there for all to see:
for politicians, politics is the art of staying
out of jail,
for convicts it is the prospect of freedom.

SUICIDE NOTE SENT BY ESENIN FROM MOSCOW

There is nothing new in dying in this city,
does living in it carry greater merit?

Translated by Feyyaz Kayacan Fergar

SHAKESPEARE IN TURKEY

Hamlet's soliloquy ended before it began!
From now on "to be or not to be"
will give way to
"not to be or not to be".

HAEMORRHOIDS AND RESURRECTION

It is not a cypress but a Judas-tree
that is standing over me. The field
is buried in me, I am buried in the field.
In this summer-struck world, I am the only corpse
to smell green. From now on this will be
my only sustained greeting:
'Hurrah', I shall say, 'hurrah for death,
hurrah for the mobilised crescendos
of all its distinguished nightingales.'

'Well put', said the Judas-tree above me,
bleeding,
bleeding all the time.

Translated by Feyyaz Kayacan Fergar

WICK

Something in me stinks.
I wash it hard, it won't wash off.

There is a mask preying on me.
I pull it hard it won't come off.

There is a child in my breast.
Death after death I die, not so the child.

There is a lighter in my eye.
Hard, I strike it hard, the flame

bursts into your faces.

Translated by Feyyaz Kayacan Fergar

WORLDLY GOODS

My eyes cannot stand this blue,
the azalea's still in flower,
I wish there was no hurt in beauty.
What's in dying? I'm ending endlessly,

I could never have enough of love.
I might become a Judas-tree on the Bosphorus.
I travelled the vast ocean of feverish hope and know now
that my heart is but a mussel.

No raki - I went straight for the cologne.
This good-for-nothing modesty is like an island.
I'm afraid the world that brought me
into this world will kill me again with love.

Translated by Richard McKane

HEY

They turned out the lights last night,
we groped for and picked up the chess pieces
and were ordered to bed.

The breaths of sleeping friends wandered
round the prison dormitory like black-as-night cats;
go on wander a little then.

I was setting fair for home,
my oars not even dripping yet,
when those screaming naked lights burst on above me.

A convict getting away from it all in a rowing boat on the
Bosphorus.
They're right of course they cannot leave me to it, but...
hey, I never knew that darkness could be so good!

Translated by Richard McKane

SEISMOGRAPHY

The world stood on the horns of an ox, said the myth.
Every move of the ox caused an earthquake.
In fact the world rests on the shoulders of the people.
See what happens if they move.

Translated by Feyyaz Kayacan Fergar

ARITHMETIC

One Turk is worth the whole world, is a saying of Atatürk.
Leaving aside the distant and recent past,
but considering the events lately
in Sebinkarahisar and Gaziantep:
that is, if what the papers say is true -
some Turks have been tortured,
for whatever reason,
they were hanged from the ceiling by their feet,
were subjected to electric shocks here and there, etc.
So I repeat, that is, if the news is true,
and if as a nation we take to heart this statement
that one Turk is worth the whole world:
we - I mean some of us
and we can't tell how many -
by torturing some of us
have committed a crime against humanity, against so many worlds -
nobody knows how many -
and against so many worlds beyond this life.

Translated by Esra Nilgün Mirze and Richard McKane

Hasan Hüseyin
(1927-84)

DICE

It's bad
things are in a bad way
things are in a very bad way
things are really bad

It's either here or there
it's either this way or that way
either today or tomorrow
either in the evening or in the morning

Things are positively in a bad way
things look very bad
yes things look bad
bad

No, it can't be said to be bad
There is always this way or the other way
or vice versa
If it happens this way ... it won't be so bad
if it happens that way it'll be good
if it happens like I said it'll be super

Good good
Things are sitting pretty
very very pretty
Really things couldn't be better

FOUL WEATHER FRIEND

I know poetry
is not water in the flask
bread in the bag
bullet in the belt.

Even so it can uphold
those without water in their canteen
without bread in their bag
without bullets in their belt.

I know this is not
a thing to be done with poetry and song.
It is not the cooing of the dove
that ripens the pomegranate on its branch
the crops in their fields

Even so poetry's task in a struggle
is to shine
like a knife
between clenched teeth

Blindness everywhere
not a single light
The heart is a wounded falcon.
spiralling in the air

Perhaps it is a poem
perhaps it is the crumb of a poem
that knocks at our door in the hopeless dark
that sounds our heart
that bends over our wound
that dispels our fear.

And from the hills opposite
a clarion's resounding call

Translated by Feyyaz Kayacan Fergar

Turgut Uyar
(1927-85)

EVERYONE

They were caught unprepared, they had long voices.
Long arms, long beards.
Whoever is woken from such sunken sleep
has to rub his eyes
like a black rabbit
in a field of carrots.
This black-eyed boy
had, with janissaries, dismissed Byzantium,
had donated his blood to conquests.
This boy had a forelock,
this boy had none.
And they, soldiers by book and uniform discarded,
they who had never worn glasses,
surgical belts,
with hunger swollen like doughnuts in their guts,
their hearts rattling with the pain of death,
they were all caught unprepared.

I know an evening tasting like an exhibition
in the midst of garrulous mouths and expensive flowers.
His love should go well with the sun,
with days gone by,
in the midst of urgent wheat and oats.

New bar of soap,
give up, for God's love, tarring my heart,
I walk barefoot in rice fields.
Many remembered the old days,
many their old fate.
Many, more or less many
were caught unprepared.

Oh death, with eyes bigger than graves,
you cannot take us in full.
Some things are bound to stay with us,
things that none can wear out:
a ripe summer evening, a how are you,
a rising with the sun like a raised cup.
The day veered from the Mediterranean, from Çukurova,
it veered into a feast till morning celebrated.
But the waters stopped, the evening grew long,
and everyone, oh how lovely, everyone
was caught unprepared.

OBRAS COMPLETAS

For Lorca

We know now for certain
blood shed in the name of the people
is like a knife
with a rosewood handle
beautiful between one's teeth
in Spain
and everywhere .....

Translated by Feyyaz Kayacan Fergar

Metin Eloğlu
(1927-85)

THINNESS OF OUR DAYS

You can no longer steal extra time
out of fate's timetable. Here we are
sunken on our knees in unison,
stained by tobacco, erased by drink.

If only we had a poem to memorise.

KNOT

I have a feeling I've seen
these bargain beauties before.
If I were to go rummage through old books
I might even burst into tears.

Shall I, shall I let my hair down?
Please do.

EROSION

I want to live
you want to live
he wants to live.

You'll say, do you call this poetry?
But what kind of world is this?
Do you call this peace?
Do you call this freedom?
Do you call this brotherly love?
I know, put up with it, you'll say.
Yes but what kind of life would that be?

Translated by Feyyaz Kayacan Fergar

Edip Cansever
(1928-85)

ALUMINIUM SHOP

I cast one look at the sea
and the fish turn into shoals of song.
I say this shoe has been worn.
I say this cheese is soaking wet,
this I say is a boiled potato in your hand.
This is man's intuition,
this, his mind.
This is the law, the law all around
just like strawberry is strawberry .....
I then say this is the truth, you too know the truth.
This is the driving of the nail,
this is the buttering of the bread,
this is the knowledge of love, of shame, of man,
this is feeling, this is thinking, this is the burden
we see in everything.
This is inside society, this is outside,
this is your situation, this is nature's doing,
this the mindless flower,
this the illiterate tree.

And here is straightforward foresight,
here the water, here the river, the wind,
the stone, the cloud.
I say this is the known and this the unknown.
Over there is BC and here is AD.
And look here comes the latest crop of newest men
boxes after boxes of modalities
twisted tin
aluminium shop.

DEDUCTION

My eyes somehow
remind me of you.

A NEW ERA

I saw this Adam (no part of him was moving)
sitting on a chair -
not quite sitting - the chair had no legs.
What have we here then, is this man in the abstract or what?
If you look you'll see he has some connection with his hands.
They are long and long and truly long,
pigheaded, intent upon love or lust.
I spoke, he didn't.
I prodded him, he wouldn't budge.
I lost my temper, swung my knife into his belly.
Well I never ...
he didn't take a blind bit of notice.

I was at a loss, I searched myself all over.
Had we walked into a new era so early in the morning?
Man doesn't model for death any more.

Translated by Feyyaz Kayacan Fergar

Cemal Süreya
(1931-90)

THE WILD SLANG OF THE HEART

You were a child, you were yet to bring
the untidy voice of your scattered words
into the wholeness of light.
This is what perhaps drove you,
leaving your shadow behind like a blue cover.

And you felt in your bruised eyes
lime-trees, warm as prophets.

Thus started the long flowing
of that first,
that prestigious,
that illiterate
water.

It was a poetry in a way:
the wild slang of the heart.

It was friendship in a way,
it could feel
the lute, drop by drop,
taking shape
in the pebble.

DECLARATION

The day of the coming of freedom:
on that day it is forbidden to die.

Fragments from "MAKE LOVE TRAVELLER"

1

With one hand
you open the door a little.
But the trembling
in the other,
is still the world's mother tongue.

2

Make love traveller, utter great words
and quickly depart.
Abysses are afoot on the highest peaks.

MANIA

Your poem is a disease of friendship:
you press a scorpion to your bosom
thinking it a lily.

OUR NIGHTS ARE SHORT

My breath is a red bird
in the auburn sky of your hair.
When I hold you in my lap
no words can describe the flow of your legs.

My breath is a red horse now
I can tell by the fire in my face.
We have nothing, our nights are short,
we must hurry, this love can't wait.

BEAUTY

Look, these are your hands, these your feet,
they are so lovely they can't be more so.
And this your hair undone since evening.

Look, this is you, my love, body and soul,
and this being a bed under us
you must have slept with me till dawn.
Listen there is no lie in me, and God is my witness,
you are so lovely that you can't be more so.

And look, these are your eyes
and their corners so used to life.
It is a good thing that they are here, what would I have
done otherwise?
Look my child, look at your arms bare and here,
our day has no secret, no recess left.
At eight in the morning your eyes dawn on me;
whatever sin we have committed it has been half and half.

Look, above all, at these, these are your lips,
they have their speaking, they have their kissing.
Softly did I kiss you with my first kiss.
We were on the boat following the shore,
three fathoms away went Istanbul.
Leaning over I softly kissed you
and close by swam the fish.

BREAKFAST

I don't know what you think on the subject of eating
but I feel there must be a connection between breakfast
and happiness.

Translated by Feyyaz Kayacan Fergar

Talat Sait Halman
(b. 1931)

SIX SHORT POEMS

1

A poet imprisoned
becomes
a thousand poets

2

Exile
is a bird
that flies each day

3

They might enslave the plant
but the seed's freedom
is limitless

4

The spring of applause
is the shortest season

5

If we have no love beyond it
we are the wall

6

I was on the brink of death.
Suddenly
a kite and a chasm
fell in love

Translated by the author

Ece Ayhan
(b. 1931)

THE DEFINITION OF OUR POETRY

Our poetry is dark, big brothers.
It wrestles with itself as soon as it hears
the sound of drum and clarinet playing by themselves.
It is peddled in dark public lavatories.
It is the poetry of young dandies in tight thingamy pinching trousers.
Love is unisons marshalled, think of it, big brothers.

Our poetry is a purple street-urchin, big brothers.
Its room is not to be found in apartments
        neatly trimmed like privet spheres.
You will hear the signal our poetry rising
        at the gates of a hired town
when a half-erased dragon with rigid semen
        and darkening lime
squats on the breath-bone of poets.
No offence, big brothers, but this was the wrong time
        to call ourselves Scutariots.*

Our poetry is core-deep in the town, big brothers.
When calendars change, a day goes missing,
a town slides into the sea of death with its dragomans.
Big brothers, how can they perpetrate such a
flat-footed town dipped in indigo emulsion?

Translated by Feyyaz Kayacan Fergar

* *Scutariots from Scutari (Üsküdar) on the shores of the Bosphorus where the poet lived for a long time.*

AN EMPTY-EYED BLACK CAT

Here comes the forgetful acrobat. The time is the late hours of the sea. He blows out the lamp. He lies down alongside my weeping side. I am crying for the prophet Daniel. Below lives a blind woman. She is in a delirium in a language unknown to me. There is a heavy butterfly on her breast. She is full of broken drawers. Auntie Sally Sad drinks high in the attic. She does embroidery too. She has been kicked out of schools where they taught the milk of human kindness. The empty-eyed black cat crosses the street, a child freshly deceased in its bag. The child's wings are sticking out of the bag. An ancestor turns up loudly, dealing in rags and bones.

Translated by Feyyaz Kayacan Fergar

Sezai Karakoç
(b. 1933)

QUATRAIN ON POETS

Life confronts you like a highwayman.
Poets shed off every bit
of skin and bone when they go
leaving behind their shrouds and poems.

SILENT MUSIC

Are you the winter sun?
You can burn but cannot warm.

If there is no middle to a river,
will it remind me of you?

The walls of your house are of stone:
is the smoke of stone as well?

The poem memorised
is the man you are expecting.

Translated by Mevlut Ceylan

Gülten Akın
(b. 1933)

SONG TO AN AGELESS WOMAN

Your face was never a rough sketch
its lines were a finished drawing.
You drew on your own face
in the midst of loves and fears and longings.
You wove satin cut woollen cloth,
you were tailor and dressmaker.
Bodies of the people fat and thin were clad
in your school pinafores and prison garb.

You weighed up praises from your daily life
against the losses of a higher one
and cursed the difference.
Perhaps now you're outside your body
in a silence
where everything even the smallest atom
arises and moves together.
From within silence a little late maybe
your woman's mother's maker's hand
will gather their needs again.
We've brought you roseleaves from the mountains
and made you a pillow.
Now rest your white head

1976

Translated by Ruth Christie

LAUGHING STOCK

A thousand times they made the man the
laughing stock.
They brought up fresh mirrors from below
the ground
and held them up to the sun inside him.
A thousand times they made the sun the
laughing stock.

So we could not truly gaze at the sun
tiny and orange and pale.
We knew that man to be God incalculable
which means so chubby and stubby and pale.

Translated by Talat S. Halman

SONG OF A DWELLER IN A HIGH-RISE BLOCK

They piled the houses high,
in front long balconies.
Far below was water
far below were trees

They piled the houses high,
a thousand stairs to climb.
The outlook a far cry
and friendships further still.

They piled the houses high
in glass and concrete drowned.
In our wisdom we forgot
the earth that was remote
and those who stayed earthbound.

Translated by Ruth Christie

Cevat Çapan
(b. 1933)

IN MEMORY OF JOHN BERRYMAN WHO JUMPED OFF HALF WAY DOWN THE ROAD

Having drowned in depressing nightmares
you used to wake up every morning
with a dream song.

You were like a tireless miner
who mines life's nuggets
from the richest vein of reality
that you'd staked out.

No heir even, that mad bullet
shot into your father's brain,
quicksilver images baked in the kiln fire
of iced alcohol revolved in your head
and you stuck your pain
like a country flower on to a Casanova smile.

You played the wise fool with your students,
the mad registered at your home,
you kept taxis waiting at the door with the clock running.
Death was a foreign professor
according to you -
then you succeeded in courting him too,
from the canyon of a steel bridge
with the dawn ashes
you gave yourself up
to the foaming ink of the Mississippi.
Your mind's freedom was your madness.

HOPE

Nadezhda, Voronezh, Osip Mandelstam.
As I learn the soft syllables
of these names by heart,
I keep seeing the plainclothes men
coming to take the poet away.
The exile you spent together;
diamond lines cut by Osip,
buried in Nadezhda's memory.
The cells, the huts,
the labour camps, the sanatorium,
the iced-over railway sleepers - all under snow.
And then - how did you lose one another?
Where did your hands loose their grip?

WINTER'S OVER

"I have studied the science of partings",
the speciality of exiles.
I have learned how a boat leaves the harbour,
how a train whistles in pain.

For years I lived on letters.
I fed myself on
smuggled tobacco, forbidden publications.
I never forgot. I never forgot.

Most of all I missed the sailing boats
in the icy loneliness of the steppe.
There were no mountains, no mountains,
so I leaned back on the winds.
Was I insane, or a captive
in the heart of darkness?
The blood dried -
I became a rose - and bloomed.

Translated by Richard McKane with the author

Hilmi Yavuz
(b. 1936)

SUMMER DIRGE

for Lorca

It is him you must have seen
(Caminando entre fusiles).

He is a mountain he, a summer he, woven with
golden plumes

and paths lighter than silk.
A heart of saffron he
and the consummate voice
of exile.

His identity : his lovely words of love,
his domain : a remnant of sad laurels
and a poem unknown.

What he does : he is a precipice he,
voicing the spray of oak

as if pushed back by the rushing sight
of a bare and steep autumn.
He had come here to crouch beside this
long

and irreversible poem.

It is him you must have seen
(Caminando entre fusiles).

A BLACKED-OUT POET

I am now a blacked-out poet
at random stopped in the street
by a curfew-cloud:
because the moon had been shining on my tongue
because griefs were found on me
(now being hunted who knows where).

I am now and always a poet
whose heart ticks with the instructions of grief.
Quick tell us here and now with those words that bleed,
point out to us those nacred beauties
(hiding who knows where).

I am now a poet condemned
to translate a rose into the safety
of a love poem. That is all I do.
Don't ask questions close the roads,
forget the summers, forget the poems
(being written who knows where).

INWARDNESS

Everything grows inward. What is a lake
but its own sunken bed? This was in the wake
of sorrows unfurling their black
and deep flags over my hull:

Everything grows inward. My body
suddenly is a country conceived:
"I am the keel of my own self".
This is what was said. The sayer
was one of the other travellers.

Everything grows inward. When the rose
is imminent in the bud,
language is on a pilgrimage to meet
the word of love waiting on the shore
of incoming autumn.
Everything grows inward. And now sorrow,
                                        sorrow
the deepest opponent.

MYSTERY

If the deceiver and the deceived
    are both woven into
    the pulse of language,
language itself shivers into autumn.
Facing the summer of the word
birds cover themselves with birds,
a leaf hums into the ear
    of another leaf

and says "to live a thing or to let it live itself, is one and the same."
Mountain long ago moved into mountains.

Which deep mountain is now
haunted by that golden-eyed phoenix?
A sorrow consults another sorrow
    behind all these wires

and the honey-woven word,
pulling away from language, asks
when the sayer and the prompter
    are both extant:

"What is it that makes me say I am *it* ?"

My master tells me, you are the poet,
have you ever picked a rose off the rose?

ROADS AND TIME

Spurred on by loneliness, you left,
hoping perhaps to reach a meeting point...

True, one can meet there, at that place...
to celebrate with rites of sorrow
things that can be found, that can be kept.
But what is it that has to be found and kept?
    Time or the Road
we keep looking for in gardens and poems?

Who can point yesterday?... Our heart is an ageing, sustained agony.
Roads in their ups and in their downs are always the colour of
despair.
The cloth I wrap you in, is Time...
You waited for a slow, complete coverage...

You were the Judas-tree
    undone now by the spoken words they put you in.

Translated by Feyyaz Kayacan Fergar

Kemal Özer
(b. 1936)

THE WRITING ON THE WALL

Write your belief with such conviction that it cannot be erased or concealed from the light of day.

Even if the wall you write on is torn down, make sure that, in the empty space left, the writing is still legible, so it may pass from eyes to hands and from hands to the walls in every street.

THE SWORD

You stretch out your hand to the day, only lifeless hours remain. You reach up to the tree, the fruit has been shaken down and removed. They have left the earth without harvest, the sky without air, the seas without water.

Seated on a rock you look and see that your wrist ends, not in a hand, but a sword.

Translated by Ruth Christie

Özdemir İnce
(b. 1936)

IN PRAISE OF MY FATHER

I praise and exalt my father
who never left me fatherless
because he gave himself a long life.

They killed him every day
sometimes at a clerk's desk
sometimes at the grocer or the çafé
they killed my father every day.

My father is a set of dead fathers
getting smaller and smaller in the mirror
getting bigger and bigger in the mirror;
they claimed he trampled on the sun,
that he failed to see the shadow.
Because he said "no"
or didn't say "yes" at appropriate moments,
they kept killing my father.

My father lived by dying.
Dying he lived long.
I'm a dying son too.
I praise and exalt my father.

Translated by Talat S. Halman

LETTER FOR YANNIS RITSOS

A letter came from Yannis Ritsos today,
written in black ink on pale yellow paper.
My hand held it with all the power it held for me.
It was also a call to water, grass, mountain,
a *ferman** written on silkiest vellum,
a seal of authority on the threshold of a heart.
A letter came from Yannis Ritsos today.
A letter is free in itself, it can be, it can look like anything.
Sometimes it is as transparent as a voice that has overcome pain.
Sometimes it is water, cool in its pitcher, waiting to be drunk.
Perhaps the face of Athena Panagulis among other faces,
my mother's hands smelling of soap among other hands,
a look towards the sea from Santorini.

A letter came from Yannis Ritsos today,
a whole world put into twenty lines.
If I were to go and knock at his door as a guest
and say: "Master, let us protect peace and freedom,
let us teach our children not to kill each other,
let us set a lively table with olive, tomato and cheese,
let us gather around a bottle of retsina, of raki
to drink to the seas, to the winds and friendship.
If you like we could open a tobacconist shop together."

I know the answer he would give, pure as my mother's milk.
That is why we celebrated an early feast with friends,
raising our glasses to the safe future of the neighbouring shore.
That is why my hands and forehead are Aegean blue.

A letter came from Yannis Ritsos today.
A poet's heart has joined the signs of the Zodiac.

Translated by Feyyaz Kayacan Fergar

* *Ferman: a royal decree*

THE STARKER THE BETTER

(From Twelve Poems for Yannis Ritsos)

A poem confiscated with flowers,
a poem in pieces cutting its lips,
a poem on the verge of the hanging tree.

This is how among ourselves
we now test and define the undefeatable.

Translated by Feyyaz Kayacan Fergar

Ülkü Tamer
(b. 1937)

POETRY

Poetry makes a new start every day.
Every morning it wakes up
to wash its words
to comb its letters.

It is fond of looking at flowing water.
It has to think of mountains.
It can't do without thinking of mountains.

It enjoys a cup of tea
a cigarette
the morning paper...

It comes out to greet its neighbours
then goes on to review people at work
enters files and documents.
It is carried on the back of porters.
It jumps on the wing of a bird
from the air examines farmsteads
enjoys the warmth of mineral ore deposits
visits places, everyman's continent.

It magnifies everything in its eye.

It reduces everything.

Peculiar is its heart
it resembles no other heart
except the heart of a poem.

Everyday it sees anew.

What a little thing it is.
It is a young man's necktie,
a girl's handkerchief,
a workman's cap.

It wouldn't be the end of the world
if it were to get lost, but only sorrow
would take its place.

Knowing this
fills it with joy.

When water mixes with earth
it turns into crops, into bread.
What happens when ashes mix with earth?
It always broods on this question.
Come midday it grows tired
goes to bed with the coming of the dark.

It is the hardest working of sleep walkers.

THE TREE

Go and get me ten penny-worth of rope
from the haberdasher's round the corner.
If it isn't enough pay the rest yourself.
I'm the one to die, you're the tailor.

Perhaps in the morning perhaps who knows when
dwindling eyes will announce
ten penny-worth of doves in the tree.
This is the embroidery you call death.

TOYS - THE HORSE

Poor children are richer in imagination
than the children of the rich
for their toys are simpler.

The rich man gives his son
high-stepping rocking-horses.
But better at neighing is
the stick in the poor child's hand.

- Oh my brother, on horseback I flew a kite.
  The kite's tail got tangled
  in the mane of my horse.
  Now from the east blows
  the mane of my kite.

THE STONE SOLDIER

What was the first toy like?
Was it made of clay, was it made of reeds?

- I made a soldier of stone
  that he would my father save.
  Then with rain
  I painted him.

  Soldier, cross the mountains tonight,
  go to the big man's cave
  and bring me my father who in the corner stands.

Translated by Feyyaz Kayacan Fergar

Ergin Günçe
(1938-83)

THE HUNTER

My heart, in your silent autumn,
do not believe the maps of today.
The earth is a flat tray
and you are at the edge,
on the shores of a delicate situation.

You are a red lantern, almost within reach,
under the driving snow.
My heart, now your mountains are lost.
The wolves and wild animals
have been forced down to the snow-whitened plains.
I see the tears that
choke back your songs.

My heart, you're in the region of the lakes.
Walk now in shady paths, please,
with a hat on your head to keep off the sun.
I can read your suffering in your eyes.
Your water jugs were broken in a fire that burned down your home.
It's as though your children were burnt to ashes.

My heart, you are more respected than I among wise people.
You are in the forests; you are a hunter.
You drink of the water. You eat of the fruit.
You want to climb just one more ridge.
You smile like a child.
You tell your dog of what life was like when you were young.

The sun sank with an orange scream.
Shotgun hold-up.
You're too far away from even your humble hut.
My heart, send a telegram to yourself.
Your last journey awaits you
and the station is deserted.

You could give yourself up at the first police station,
leave your dog in the care of a friend
bury your cartridges in a corner of the forest.
You could send your notebooks to a museum.
You've lived on the run for so many years
played the Robin Hood.

If you want my opinion, I would say that
each of your loves, each of your sadnesses
you have celebrated in action.
Your rose briar pipe
your jasmine cigarette-holder
are not for the bazaar stall:
let them be for all other hunters to remember you by.

1982 (his last poem)

Translated by Gülay Yurdal Michaels and Richard McKane

Cahit Zarifoğlu
(1940-87)

BON APPÉTIT

we are a nation of artists
death comes suddenly to all of us

we eat, we leave the table
grateful for God's love and bounty
we leave the table, scimitar in hand,
before we kill intimate friends and foes
we must wash our hands first, this is a must
we must brush our teeth first, this is also a must
to do otherwise would be sacrilege

Translated by Mevlut Ceylan

Egemen Berköz
(b. 1941)

BY WAY OF EXPLANATION

Memories are for hanging on the wall,
to be looked at every now and then
when they manage to catch our eyes.
They could easily be forgotten. We show them
to guests who help us rekindle
things of the fading past.

Memories are for hanging on the wall,
men are for the hanging tree.
You do not look at them. You do not forget them.
The denizens of the hanging-tree
are no joke. They must be taken seriously.

People are dedicated to hanging-trees,
people are shot at dawn,
some people are quickly destroyed
in the middle of streets.

And some people are made to die
inch by inch
in the torture chambers
of their jobs.

QUATRAIN

When the time comes death too shall be a memory,
this will also be the day when leaves
burst through concrete and baked earth rejoins Earth itself.
Surely this is the time to write a new poem.

Translated by Feyyaz Kayacan Fergar

Melisa Gürpinar
(b. 1941)

From "SUMMER SEQUENCE"

XXXIII

my eyes search everywhere for the hunter
the hunting season about to arrive
gunfire
a warm wingful in the cool of morning
will take me from myself
how much I see myself a partridge

I know the land of death is hid in mist
no face to be seen no track to follow
no scream in the skies
and in the redbrick house of life
no one but unborn children remain

turn my partridge I said to myself turn back
it is your fear that colours your feathers
as you stumble through the reeds
how can you know the hunter
like a friend who forgot you
clothed in silence
it's he who is waiting perhaps his finger on the trigger

day is short the way endless
everything is trapped in night
the sun throws itself in the lake
like a waterfly ending its life

Translated by Ruth Christie

Ataol Behramoğlu
(b. 1942)

THE UNLIT STREETS OF THE POOR

As I carry my string bag of shopping in the evenings
through the unlit streets of the poor
my mental weariness lifts, and all the way home
like a red rose in the worn hands of a flowerseller in the road

the feeling warms my heart
that I can sing the poetry of my people.

THE SCREAM*

Was this the time to murder a man, gunning him down
just when he'd kissed his child and stepped to the door?

The spring day trampled and bloodied
suddenly covered its face with a scream of shame,

a scream like a shrivelled rose, like hope abandoned,
the joyous human life choked in the noose of wire.

Rain softly falling lamented to the night.
The scream. At the window the face of a child.

Translated by Ruth Christie

* *When writing this poem, Ataol, I think, had in mind the days of the 'slow motion civil war' in Turkey when people use to be kidnapped and shot all over the place. It has the quality of a film with terrifying close-ups, especially the face of the child witness at the window. - F.K.F.*

POEM WRITTEN ON THE EVE OF MY FORTIETH YEAR

I must put an end to shoddy enthusiasms
because I am the same age as the wind
because the sun is my brother
because the river and I are lovers.

I should really lead a cool, calm life.
I should really pare off all pretence and affectation
but the thing is the beauty of poetry
competes in my heart with the joy of life ...

I must put an end to trivial worries and passions
because I am the same age as the world
because I am riding on the lovely crest of an eddying flux
that has no beginning, no end.

Translated by Feyyaz Kayacan Fergar

QUATRAIN

I don't think the thought of death
would have scared me much.
What hurts and bothers my pride
is being caught between two dates.

FOR A SONG BY THEODORAKIS *

Only a woman whose lover
was killed could sing such a song.
Crying has dried up all the roots of her tears,
but faith in the days to come
is still the greenest strength in her heart.

Translated by Feyyaz Kayacan Fergar

* *Mikis Theodorakis, the Greek composer, who has always been popular in Turkey.*

İsmet Özel
(b. 1944)

LINES WRITTEN ON THE BACK OF THE LAST PICTURES I HAD TAKEN OF ME WHILST I WAS SMILING AT MY EXECUTIONER

I am Ismet Özel, a poet in his fortieth year.
Everything happened in my lifetime, I want this
to be known by all. I was there when the deluge came
I was present at the re-creation of the world.
I am at peace now, I have seen everything.
I saw the parting of the heavens, the coming to life of clay.
All the evidence is at hand now. I can be lynched.
I earned the hatred of prostitutes
and the curses of virgins.
I have words which can't even help you cross a bridge,
I have words which will not save you from burning fires.
I have lost the sword of my strength, I no longer
respect harvests. I flew but my flight
was detected by radar. I swore heavily:
this too was entered in my police file.

Let everyone know, I am quite a hooligan.
Gendarmes and taxmen are after my soul.
In the eyes of the clockwork toilers,
nothing could be blacker than my soul;
if you ask the denizens of laboratories
my soul is a fake.
All the youngsters who sailed through school
with flying colours and an eye for what is true
will tell you that my soul is a slovakian snail
whose home was left in Nepal.
I wonder who knows the truth.

Even I, busy as I am hiding my soul
in every crack and cranny
what do I know?   What do I possess
that could possibly tempt the devil down my throat?
Dishevelled by anxiety, I selected a state secret
for myself.   With a state secret in hand
one could lead a cinematic life,
one could enjoy refined living,
those secret trips to the fleshpots
of whore-houses, not to mention
high-class restaurants or simple bucolic walks.
Who knows, it might all end
on the platform of an aesthetic execution.
Yes, yes, but a soul is not enough
to rake in all these goodies.

If this verdict,
this conclusion,
this inference is right,
why is it that a conference postponed
or a late coach
muddles everything,
why are the trains of national leaders always white,
why are the Russians marching on Berlin?

How absurd, how stupid!
Of the four bibles why do I choose to follow
the gospel according to John?

But here I am,
one out of many, like everyone else
standing at this station
next to this spy in his black coat
waiting with my most legible face.
I stay in the game, I play it
for fear that I might miss my turn,
that my ticket might expire.
There are heaps of azaleas
and passion flowers lying before me
like corpses with rigid valves,
there are thousands of flowers before me.

I am afraid it might be my cue to step in:
what if they tell me to begin in order to make an end?
Oh no, not to me,
the world mustn't do this to me.
Tell me, when all is said and done
how many of us went as close as seeing
their own skeleton in the mirrors?

Come now, humanity,
let's strike a bargain:
give me all the derelict thoughts
you left behind,
all the days you deserted, your past mistakes
all the moments of despair triggered
by your shortcomings, give them all to me,
give me your sorrows, the jokes you no longer
find funny, all the things you think
you have quelled, give them, give them to me,
the worries you tried to make light of, all the fallen,
broken dreams and the wild, failed ventures,
give them all to me,
give me also your crimes
documented with their entire premeditations.
I know, it wouldn't be
the done thing if I were
to hand out a cheque in exchange,
money is too coarse a unit
to measure the intricacies
of all these sustained plunders.
Look, apart from my usual tricks
I can find other interesting ways of repayment.
When it comes to repayment I am a peerless expert.
For instance, what would you say
to a lecture at one of your club's meetings?

A lecture: on the shining ideals of humanity.
Or else I could arrange a raffle on your behalf.
With vertigos, nostalgias
and festering loves to be shared
by prize winners.

Let a just bargain be struck
at long last!
Against all your past offences
I have lined up all the crimes
I intend to commit.
No matter what I do
I'll have to bear the brunt
of every impregnating, pestilent wind.

If still waters cry deep
let them run into me.
The forging strength of fire
and the wisdom of earth
shall not fail to restore
my sword to me.

Translated by Feyyaz Kayacan Fergar

Güven Turan
(b. 1944)

WHEEL OF FORTUNE

This word shall remain rooted
in deepest blankness
till the next word is ushered in
to spell the pregnant apex of wholeness:
- an utterly white moon
  ghosted by white nights

- an utterly blank wind
  in utterly pale augusts

- an utterly white dream
  erased by nakedness.

Magnify all this, add to it
increasingly, the starkness,
the lack of voice and smell
of all the things whose touch
leave our body deeply unmoved.

Everything lives in a spectrum of blankness
here, on the blurred lips of memory.

EXPECTATIONS

How far can I go
standing crucially still?
This question stalks my loving,
my meals, the signature
I put at the end of a letter.
What is stranded here as a day postponed
is what should have been lived long years ago.
I know the logic,
I know how to make today
tomorrow's dumb hostage.

Petty quarrels do not unveil life
and its great definitions,
whereas it is always the lull
that precedes the storm.

FORCE OF HABIT

Under his pillow
he leaves reminders from the night before.
The morning starts breezy and clear.
He strolls quietly about,
he is noiseless, he comes
to squat over his diary,
a mystery to him
and open book for others.

His entries run through
a flight of pages, then comes
the renewal of night,
the coming again of dark sleep
weaving the deep sinews of sleeplessness.

Translated by Feyyaz Kayacan Fergar

Özkan Mert
(b. 1944)

From "TANGO AND GOD"

I

I am a shining exile
loneliness is my head-teacher.
They hanged my heart
between Turkey and the world.

II

I made this wine from the heart
of the grapes that were the first to see the sun on earth.
I wash my words with this wine,
history is looking for me.

III

It could be that poetry is a pirate,
a crimson-bearded robber of time.

IV

Like broken pieces of a mirror
we shall reflect each other
and multiply from shard to shard.

V

Nobody was able to prove
that the world was not ruled by love -
not even Marx.

VI

How much longer are they going to torture
the young? Are students to pay
for history in their cells?
The arms are silent. Can we hear democracy?

Translated by Feyyaz Kayacan Fergar

Refik Durbaş
(b. 1944)

SOMEONE

My flute was frail, my head was fertile,
and played a new dance every evening,
but as I walked in the high meadow on the longest day
adding fortune telling to coffee cups and silence
it turned into my barbarous voice
filled it deep and trembling
and loaded its own gun.

My heart became the soul of a lilac,
accommodated rancour and gently blew
into my medicated lungs that the bayonets had pierced
one evening when I was seeking shelter.
Now the day has long died on which I can tell
someone of my desperation. There are sounds in the depths,
in the depths of finished and forgotten loves,
all and everyone in the crowding in depths.

Now the blood fades on my lips,
my flute is sharp and angry.
I'm tired. I've forgotten how to play it.
I should go. My heart dances fast,
but where is my love? I have forgotten
I have forgotten whom I can tell
of my desperation.

Translated by Richard McKane

MY NAME

Write my name by the side of the field of flowers
blossoming in abysses.

Translated by Feyyaz Kayacan Fergar

ANNIVERSARY

Mountains have been raising hopes, never orphans.
Ever since the day you came
with flowering rifle and soaring refusal
to steal death out of the festering jaws of treachery.
Oh brother of my breath, sun of my eyes, core of my mind,
do no longer condemn your anger to silence.

The day of belief has come round again
let us once more celebrate this anniversary.

THE SPARROWS

With joy he rushed out into the street.
It was morning - he went through
the whole length of the town
shattering all the windows
of the houses.
He changed the place of the streets.
He changed the place of the sorrow in his heart,
the address of loneliness.

There were sparrows flying in his hair:
them he did not touch.

POEM 94

Is there no other smell than fear
in this town?

POEM 99

The fire is in the attic of my skull,
the rain in the pupils of my eyes.
Go now, let me see to my death.

Translated by Feyyaz Kayacan Fergar

Sennur Sezer
(b. 1944)

MORNING SONG

Listen!
The morning has three doors in the sky.
One of them is hope.
Take it and give it to the child
let him grow with it
let him grow tall and walk tall.

Listen, listen!
The morning has three doors in the sky.
One of them is the daily bread
shining in your hands.
Let it shine on and increase
all the bright way long.

Listen, I say, listen!
The morning has three doors to the sky.
One of them is fear.
Silence it!
The bread is yours, the hope is yours.
What can fear do
when hands can speak unto other hands?

Translated by Feyyaz Kayacan Fergar

Nihat Behram
(b. 1946)

WISH FROM THE EAST

Feed me with the horror of the past
with the juice and sap of the future

Hang cherries on my ears as earrings
wash my kerchief with basil herb

Impress on my memory the crazy thunder
let the echoing nights close on me

Introduce me to the winds
tie my eyes to the storm

Know that I am the blood brother of your tears
cast a spell on me with your hope

Give me shooting stars in the desert of the night
make me the point between two flints rubbing together

Rain on my breast the rain that washes the ears of wheat
invigorate my groin with olive leaves

I shall take you captive with poems
know that I am your slave

Translated by Richard McKane

Ismail Uyaroğlu
(b. 1948)

THE HOLLYHOCK

Three thousand species of trees
and bushes are said to belong to the rose family
but not the hollyhock, though its flowers
equal the rose in beauty and hue.
It is relegated to the level of the mallow.
The poet is a bit like the hollyhock.
He is locked out of the family of man
but more human than the whole lot.

NEVER

To think of a flower drawing
a knife on poetry is feasible.
But it is unthinkable to imagine
a poem knifing a flower.

INDELIBLE

The wind that blows on the right of my forehead
cannot erase the hell that rages on the left.

SEA AND POETRY

The sea is a poet in blue
who writes magic poems.
Stand by the shore,
empty all the words
into the palm of your hand.
Look a little later,
you'll see the white spray
of poetry breaking over the rocks.

Translated by Feyyaz Kayacan Fergar

Bariş Pirhasan
(b. 1951)

THE HEARTLESS LAKE

I reached the shore of a lake.
Bending over its mirror I said:
"Will you give me a drop to drink?"
I am sleepy, said the lake.

I turned into a small stream.
Fast I flowed up the mountain
to reach the shore of the lake
but found its eyes closed tight.

I stole stars from the night
to brighten its shore.
"Why do you bring these,
I am heavy with salt," said the lake.

I shed my clothes on the sand,
bending over its mirror, I asked
"Will you cry with me?"
"I am sleepy," said the lake.

Fragment from "HISTORY IS EVIL"

There they are, the poems of my youth,
the handsome utterances
of those early years,
a time of clumsy but fine nonsense.
I must have written them
with sensual, tremulous fingers ....

All these now belong to the past.
But what I wrote as child gives me courage.
Like an idiot,
like all destitute people
I plot rebellion
in a dazed handwriting.

Translated by Feyyaz Kayacan Fergar

Turan Koç
(b. 1952)

RECORD

look youth is not repeatable
what we carry on our shoulders is our burial ground
there are children who cry on our doorsteps
by invitation we are prone to deadends

after all the doings all the sayings
our women will have to make do
with a flower-spoken precipice

FULL DAY

how would I know
the centre of a poem, the heart of a loaf,
the taste of calm weathers in my mouth,
how would I know
how many springs, how many pictures
I have in my pocket?

this afternoon is humming in me,
your eyes are huge, shadowy.
walk, let the streets stretch
walk, let your motherhood increase.
something light, something airy rises in me.
how would I know
whether it's love or helplessness?

Translated by Mevlut Ceylan

Arif Ay
(b. 1953)

HERE

the wind blows quietly
a tile falls into the garden
the sun looks at my hand
a raindrop falls in my tea
a cloud like a ship slowly
draws up to my table
hand in hand we climb up
to the deck of the evening

here are the stars we say
we repeat the names of flowers
later as though nothing has happened
you feed the chickens first thing in the morning

Translated by Mevlut Ceylan

Tuğrul Tanyol
(b. 1953)

SWALLOW DAYS

My swallow days! Who can reach
your scents of mint and thyme?
Rain is only a memory,
light and shade play on the dirty wall of night
and slowly dissolve in the light's fragile porcelain bowl.

My swallow days! the scent of mint and thyme dissolve
and the sediment in the waters within me settles.
A seagull's wings catch fire. The secret notebook
of memories catches fire into red and blue flames.

My swallow days! When a child
hurtles out of the history of mirrors,
his faded blue eyes piercing and questioning,
the ash-grey rock of the day splits,
silver threads and embroidery fall apart.
Say this to him: 'Don't forget.
The spring map is drawn and redrawn.'

My swallow days! You...
How you have flown by.

Translated by Richard McKane

BASRA

The dead calm gulf's waters drew back.
The crazed stallion of desire got mad.
Autumn rushed into the gully of a shivering summer
like a snake rearing away from its black shadow.

Ah, the leaf that curls with pain and trembling happiness.
Is this a crumb of thought that brings life
to a feeling in an enigma? The total absence shattering
the sacred dust in the vast emptiness - perhaps a moonstone
perhaps that Satrap of darkness cloaked in green
from distant Kerbela, on the haj to Mecca,
in pillaged and looted Basra city.

Medieval, with a white beard and black turban
he seeps into the dead calm gulf's waters.
Die, kill and be blessed
on the field where the crescent is split in two.

My God, where is the promised key to paradise.
The dark waters of the gulf bear away
the ownerless shadows of the purple corpses

Translated by Richard McKane

THE WIND

When my eyes are averted I can hear
the wind at the back of my house
but when I look, silence is everywhere.

Outside the window, the branch of a tree:
the wind hidden and ripe in the stone of every fruit.

Translated by Feyyaz Kayacan Fergar

AUTUMN ENDING

Candles melt one by one
        and quietly die in my body
At the touch of autumn
        gold veers to copper.

Where are you now? I waited so long
my leaves are exhausted.
The wind stole drops from the heart of the clouds,
took hold of me,
        pursued me,
made me go through the rusty paths
        of my youth.

Autumn was just a coincidence
but the tree couldn't tell.

With every rain we age a bit more.
Does the cloud know that?
This dread, this alarm churning up
        the depths of the sea,
                this face,
abandoned in mirrors,
this hustle and bustle?   Who are they for?

One day the rock of silence will split,
one day this wandering wind will settle on our head
and storms find peace in swallows' wings.

And copper shall voice the gold
and rain the ancestral cloud.

Translated by Feyyaz Kayacan Fergar

MEETING

And I took my body and carried it to far mountains.
I made myself shrink, shrink down almost
to the size of a dot. They came to handle me,
to place me over some impossible letters,
making up words where no love dwelt ...

And all I wanted was to go out and meet the remnants
of an autumn lingering in our eyes,
and the losses of our hearts.

CEREMONY

The weather is priceless, who cares about ceremonies?
This train, cutting itself loose, will pack its clouds
and go. Hey, uncle, don't forget your speech.
We'll listen to it when we come back.

But we could change our minds.

Translated by Feyyaz Kayacan Fergar

Yaşar Miraç
(b. 1953)

LIKE A DREAM

In a tiny house
with almond windows
sugar-melon doors
on fish legs
in a cool house
with cherry curtains
in the summer heat
in a house with little flowers
in the winter cold
in a house where inspiration is a dawn breeze
in the beautiful countryside
in a small house
on a September night
in a tiny house
with a silver smile
in a plum house
I too would like to live
to live and live with you.

Translated by Richard McKane

Hüseyin Avni Dede
(b. 1954)

PRISON SONG

He leans
his head slightly
my head
touches
the stars

love flows
from the marrow
of the night

outside
it grows
of its own accord
and inside also

IF A LETTER COMES MY EYES WILL LOOK DIFFERENT

If a letter comes from my love, if she calls me to her,
if I take the early road to the village,
if she sees me at the door, and shouts to me,
if I kiss, embrace her and hold her hand;

then lullabied by the night, I'll put love to sleep,
and if at last I find a new job -
swallowing razor blade on razor blade in the circus,
I would forget singing and playing the violin.

Translated by Richard McKane

Mevlut Ceylan
(b. 1958)

PREY

A knife in my veins
pursues its prey;

in my flesh
invoices, owls
and earthquakes;

in my dreams
so many lives
so much learning and death.

The knife never sleeps

SEEKING

When my muscles swelled with the weight
of love
I laid my mind on the ground.

In the farthest corners of the world
they found me on top of a mountain
chasing the moon and stars.

Bending my forefinger
as though pulling the trigger
I let fly the bird from three hills.

Translated by Ruth Christie

Nevzat Çelik
(b. 1961)

I'M TALKING TO YOU

Take this pen from my hand, take the bleeding words.
I'm talking of death, don't you understand, raise your heads,
raise your heads high, don't stay outside, don't let winter multiply
on the threshold.
Oh my god is that wild-garbed dawn opening up at five again?

Don't let them blind the skylarks, don't let the poets die young.
what season are we in, did it snow on your hair?

I can't see a branch which stays green for four seasons.
Do you know the sadness of a girl who's an open flower that has not
been smelled?

Why doesn't the cloud cry for the child's lost balloon?
Why do fire and gunpowder run to each other out of desperation?
Hey Hasan hey Hasan Hüseyin are these pangs forbidden me?
What does one have to do to make waiting bad and living good?

February 1983-January 1984

KEEP MY NIGHTS WARM

My parting is temporary.
I'm pregnant with a first summer flower.
Don't trot out the laments in my name
I didn't die, I will not die.

Keep my nights warm.
I'll come out from under the snow.
I'll blow like a hot wind
from the fire of your dreams.

Put on the strong tea
feed the stove like a hungry child.
The smoke puffs in my eyes
like incense clouds.

Make my bed long
so my toes don't stick out
at night - Lord have mercy -
I'll gently curl up and sleep.

My dear dear friends
is my place ready in the bosom of your family?
There'll come a day when I'll come along
shouting and screaming like a child who's late.

December 1982

Translated by Richard McKane

Necati Polat
(b. 1962)

LET ME BE, GENTLEMEN

you cannot tie me down to this city
side by side with your own kind
my breath quickened into death
my heart was swindled
you cannot tie me down to this city

I cover myself with the soft skins of poems
but you want to prey on that as well
you cannot tie me down to this city
let me be, gentlemen
do I look like a professional slave
what use am I to you anyway

I am a bit of a spoilsport, gentlemen
I've got a bit of a barking pen
with a bit of a bite as well, gentlemen
you cannot tie me down to this city

Translated by Mevlut Ceylan

Kemal Kalé
(1960-90)

MIGRANT

Following the wind, the songster of freedom,
I am on my way to the rainbows' secret dwellings,
an enduring morning at my side.

BIOGRAPHY

The flower of dreams blossomed, multiplied in a street
of shadows, then decayed into rebirth in the air.
Only the rain and the wind felt this.

THE MIRROR OF SORROWS

The sky is the colour of shame
what has it seen this time?
A darkness settles around the blue
                    of its eyes.

Translated by Feyyaz Kayacan Fergar